THE EDGES OF THE FIELD

The Edges of the Field

Lessons on the Obligations of Ownership

JOSEPH WILLIAM SINGER

BEACON PRESS

BOSTON

Beacon Press
25 Beacon Street
Boston, Massachusetts 02108-2892
www.beacon.org

Beacon Press books
are published under the auspices of the Unitarian Universalist
Association of Congregations.

Printed in the United States of America
05 04 03 02 01 00   8 7 6 5 4 3 2 1

This book is printed on acid-free paper
that meets the uncoated paper
ANSI/NISO specifications for permanence as revised in 1992.

Text design by Lucinda Hitchcock
Composition in Bembo by Wilsted & Taylor Publishing Services

LIBRARY OF CONGRESS CATALOGING-IN-PUBLICATION DATA
Singer, Joseph William.
The edges of the field : lessons on the obligations of ownership /
Joseph William Singer.
p.   cm.
ISBN 0-8070-0438-3 (cl: acid-free paper)
1. Property—United States.   2. Right of property—United States.   3. Property—Moral
and ethical aspects.   4. Right of property—Moral and ethical aspects.   I. Title.
KF572.S57   2000
330.1'7—dc21   00-024633

For

Marcel Pallais

זכרון צדיק לברכה

ובקצרכם את־קציר ארצכם לא תכלה פאת שדך
לקצר ולקט קצירך לא תלקט: וכרמך לא תעולל
ופרט כרמך לא תלקט לעני ולגר תעזב אתם אני
יהוה אלהיכם:

ויקרא יט:ט

*When you reap the harvest of your land, you shall not reap all
the way to the edges of your field, or gather the gleanings of
your harvest. You shall not pick your vineyard bare, or gather
the fallen fruit of your vineyard; you shall leave them for the
poor and the stranger: I am the Lord your God.*

—Lev. (*Vayikra*) 19:9

Contents

Do not, any of you, oppress your brother or your sister.
                                          — Lev. (*Vayikra*) 25:14

Property rights serve human values. They are recognized to that end, and are limited by it.[1]
                                          — Chief Justice Joseph Weintraub
                                          Supreme Court of New Jersey,
                                          State v. Shack

We live in a time when the national economy, by many measures, is doing very well. But we also live in a time when many people, by other measures, are doing quite poorly. We have "reformed" welfare by getting rid of it for many families who will continue to need help. We have created fabulous wealth while increasing inequality. We have seen the rise of new information-based industries and the collapse of manufacturing and the family farm. We have seen great advances in civil rights, but in many ways we are more segregated by race and class than in the past. The distribution of both wealth and income remains highly unequal among racial and ethnic groups. Women have new opportunities but continue to earn less than men and to bear the double burden of working both outside and inside the home. According to federal standards, about 20 percent of our children are living in poverty; among African-American children, the figure is almost 50 percent.[2] Single mothers and their children are very likely to be poor, even if the mothers are working outside the home. Job opportunities abound for many, but not for everyone — especially those in the inner city — and often not for wages that would sustain a family. The stock market is soaring and so is the practice of downsizing. A rising tide may lift all boats, but some people have no boats, and they are drowning.

Americans have always valued self-reliance, but it is not all we value. Self-reliance, as an ideal, can invoke the sense that each person is important. What you think matters; what you choose to do will determine whether your life is a story or a farce. But self-reliance, as an ideology, can collapse into solipsism. A romantic view of self-reliance can easily become a justification for glorifying self-interest. If we are entitled to no help from others, it is a small step to believing that we are justified in considering our own interests without regard to the needs of others. As Jedediah Purdy notes, we live in "a time whose characteristic excesses are mutual indifference and the seductive illusion of self-reliance."[3]

Yet indifference to others is not a high value in our culture. Our religious leaders, our teachers, our movies, our television shows, our popular music, even our political leaders, all counsel us not to be selfish. In those moments when we think about our deepest values, we feel the pull of something that takes us out of ourselves. When we are at prayer, when we are with family, when we face a deadly illness, when we confront a disaster, we derive comfort and meaning from the belief that what we do matters. To be a human being – to act humanely – is not to think of yourself alone.

Despite this, we live in a time when looking out for yourself has become the cornerstone of public policy. The "public interest" is almost a quaint concept. Welfare as "we have known it" is a thing of the past. Personal responsibility is our watchword. I have no problem with the idea of responsibility. I do have a quarrel with the notion that we are entitled to be indifferent to the fate of others and that we cannot rely on anyone but ourselves. Self-reliance is a good thing but it is not the only good thing. No one has made it in America on their own. Tax cutting and deregulation are fine if they leave in place familial, social, economic, and legal institutions that provide the support and opportunity that people need to take care of themselves and their families. For many people, those supports are gone. Rather than promoting personal responsibility, we are creating many harried, overworked, underpaid people who are struggling to find enough time and resources to take care of their families. This has got to stop.

Americans are really very compassionate, but recent public policy has not reflected this. Too many people today are running in place or falling behind, despite their best efforts. Too often, the only response from our political leaders is to deregulate even further, the better to encourage people to work even harder. There is another way. I believe our political course can reflect our empathetic values while protecting individual liberty and providing for economic growth. The current divide between our caring impulses and our political norms must be bridged.

This book explores the cultural, moral, religious, and legal traditions that help define our understanding of private property. Contrary to what some believe and others fear, the protection of property rights does not commit us to the view that gross inequality is a necessary fact of life or that individuals have no legitimate claim to lean on other people. Property is not merely an individual right, and it is not based solely on the notion of self-interest or self-reliance. It is, in fact, an intensely social institution.[4] It implicates social relationships that combine individualism with a large amount of communal responsibility. We value self-reliance, but we also value looking out for others. We praise those who are not selfish, who look beyond themselves. We are committed, not to indifference, but to compassion, empathy, fellow feeling. Those commitments are present in popular culture, in a variety of religious traditions, and even in American law.

Chapter 1 introduces the story of Aaron Feuerstein. When his textile factory burned down, he reacted with uncommon decency. Motivated by his religious commitments, Feuerstein not only promised to rebuild the factory, but announced that he would pay his workers their wages for as long as he could afford to do so, and that he would do his utmost to rehire all of them. His concern for his workers and for the economic stability of his community made Feuerstein a national hero. He was held up by religious leaders and politicians alike as a model for business managers everywhere.

The paradox, however, is that he was often praised but rarely imitated. In fact, both our current business culture and our legal rules discourage other executives from following his example. We expect corporate managers to maximize profits and to further the interests of the shareholders without regard to the needs of employees or the communities in which businesses operate. And the law promotes this single-minded pursuit of profit over all other ends. This is something about which we feel deeply ambivalent. It is that ambivalence I want to explore.

Chapter 2 examines the American theory and practice of private property. The protection of private property is a core element of our law and culture. It may therefore be surprising to many people to learn that, in crucial ways, the law protects the interests of nonowners as well as owners. It protects nonowners both by limiting the legal rights of owners and by ensuring that ownership rights are defined in ways that allow nonowners to become owners. In addition, the law recognizes the burdens as well as the benefits of ownership. There are many obligations imposed on owners to use their property in ways that do not harm the legitimate interests of others or the community as a whole. The questions for us are how to accommodate conflicting interests that arise between businesses, their employees, and the public, and what the distribution of security and vulnerability should be.

Chapter 3 canvasses religious sources, starting with the core aspects of Jewish law and ethics that motivated Feuerstein and provided both the impetus and the contours of his sense of obligation. Those teachings are not unique. They are shared in different forms by both Christianity and Islam. Understanding the teachings of the major American religions about property may provide some insight into our deepest values. It may be helpful to remind ourselves what the Jewish, Christian, and Moslem traditions have to say about the proper relationship between wealth and caring obligation.

In Chapter 4, I consider images of property in popular culture. One of the stock stories in both movies and popular songs is the struggle of ordinary people against big businesses that pursue profit at any cost. This popular theme puts audiences on the side of David against Goliath. Cultural productions often capitalize on popular intuitions that reject the rapacious pursuit of profit at the expense of human suffering. I will give a number of examples from popular movies. Audiences respond to stories that implicitly or explicitly criticize economic actors who violate widely shared norms of fairness, mutual obligation, and common decency. I will then analyze in depth a highly successful cultural production, Jonathan Larson's rock opera *Rent*. Apparently striking a responsive chord among audiences across the country, the long-running production revolves around the question of what obligations we have to each other when times get rough. It develops the connections between suffering and property and suggests hints of redemption.

Chapter 5 presents some principles that could guide public policy to better support those who are at the margins of economic life. People want to respond to need, but they worry that public or communal responses will inevitably backfire, threatening liberty, individual initiative, and economic prosperity. This worry is understandable but mistaken. We do not need to tie our own hands. We can implement collective responses to need without threatening either liberty or prosperity. Our culture, our religions and our law sustain the virtues of mutual support. Implementation of those felt obligations in public policy will jeopardize neither our economic system nor our legal rights. The law today is less compassionate than people are, but it does not have to be. The law should enable the free market and productive industry, but there is no single framework for a market system. Many different property institutions are compatible with underlying norms of freedom, equality, and efficiency. It is up to us to shape our system to exhibit the values we want to live by.

In that light, I will suggest some principles that should govern public policy affecting access to property and to economic well-being. The law should both allow and encourage business managers to act in ways that take the legitimate interests of workers and communities into account when they formulate corporate policy. Public policies should enable individuals to support their families. We can and should protect the most vulnerable among us in times of economic distress. We should work through public channels to restore a fair distribution of the benefits and burdens of economic life. Our compassion can undergird our property rules rather than stop at the door of public policies.

When I was thirteen I studied a portion of the Torah — the Bible's first five books of Moses — in preparation for my bar mitzvah. It was from *Vayikra* — the Book of Leviticus — and describes the *Yovel*, the Jubilee Year in which everyone who has lost their land due to debt is entitled to return home to their land and to their families. The legal system described in the Torah protects property, but it also mandates obligations of mutual support and periodic redistribution. The moral system embedded in the Torah ensures that each person in the community — each and every one — has access to the means for a dignified human life.

I have been thinking about this Torah portion for a long time. Personal responsibility is desirable but so are the virtues of respect and compassion. The law protects what the haves have acquired, but it also created the conditions that enabled them to become owners. The have-nots should be entitled to legal rules and economic institutions that allow them to become haves. The haves should not turn away from those being left behind in this prosperous economy. It wouldn't be right.

CHAPTER ONE

Uncommon Decency

Where there are no human beings, be human.[1]
— *Hillel, Talmudic teacher*

*God may tell [Rachel] to hold back her tears; but it is just her
refusal to do this, to "be comforted," that constitutes the work
of faith in this world.*[2]
— *Avivah Gottlieb Zornberg,* Genesis

Just before Christmas 1995, the Malden Mills textile factory in Lawrence, Massachusetts, suffered a devastating fire. When the flames finally died down, three of the nine buildings were in ruins. The next
day, the owner, Aaron Mordecai Feuerstein, assembled the workers in
the high school gymnasium. They feared the worst. Most of the textile mills in New England had long ago moved to other parts of the
country, other parts of the world. Feuerstein was seventy years old and
might be ready to call it a day. The workers wondered if he would collect the insurance money and retire. What was going to happen to
them?

More than three thousand people worked for Malden Mills and
their prospects looked bleak. Then Feuerstein got up to speak. To their
astonishment, he announced that he would rebuild the factory and
that he would rehire every worker who wanted a job. He would
continue to pay their wages for the next month and they would each
receive their expected $275 Christmas bonus on time. Pandemo-
nium broke out in the gymnasium. It is reported that "grown men
cried, and in the several languages of the largely immigrant workforce — Portuguese, Spanish, Québecois — prayers of thanksgiving
were said."[3]

Feuerstein made good on his promises. Not only that: He continued to pay his workers' salaries for several more months, until he could no longer afford to do so.[4] He had no legal obligation to pay these salaries or to help his employees get through the down time. The factory was rebuilt. As of 1998, almost all the workers had been rehired.[5] And although he laid off three hundred workers because a part of the business had become unprofitable, he promised to try to rehire them within two years and provided an unusually generous package of benefits for those who lost their jobs, including extended health benefits, an extra month's pay, job retraining, and job placement assistance.[6] When he has had to lay off workers, he has done what he can to rehire them. He is committed to creating jobs in his community. Because of his actions, the town of Lawrence avoided a potential economic calamity. For the individual workers and their families, Feuerstein's actions were a godsend.

A godsend indeed. When he was asked why he did it, Feuerstein replied that he felt morally obligated. "The workers are depending upon me. The community is depending upon me. My customers are depending upon me. And my family."[7] He knew that his actions would have consequences far beyond himself. "There was no way I was going to take about 3,000 people and throw them in the street. There was no way I was going to send the city of Lawrence into economic oblivion."[8] And why not? "Because," he said, "it wouldn't be right."[9]

As an Orthodox Jew, Feuerstein relied on traditional Jewish teachings about the moral obligations of property owners. Feuerstein answered questions about his actions by quoting a Talmudic saying of the great Jewish teacher Hillel. "Where there are no men, be a man."[10] Alternatively, "When all is moral chaos, this is the time for you to be a *mensch*."[11] *Mensch* is a Yiddish word with no English equivalent. Its literal meaning is "man" or "human being" but when we say someone is a *mensch* we mean a compassionate, caring person, a person of integrity and honor, a good person who does the right thing, someone who looks out for others, someone whose actions warm your heart, someone you wish you were like.

The reaction to Feuerstein's announcement was swift and heartfelt. Editorials praised him. Religious leaders lauded him in their sermons. As the fire occurred just before Christmas, many editorials and sermons remarked on the appropriateness of his actions in that season. He was called a "Jewish Santa Claus" and a "Christmas hero."[12] In an age beset by downsizing, Feuerstein stood out. He believed he could be a good businessman and a good person at the same time. He did not segregate the values of the marketplace from his religious values. "God is one, which means to me there is one ethical standard," said Feuerstein. "The God in Lawrence is the same as the God in the marketplace, and there is one standard for us all."[13] He regretted the fact that his actions were so atypical. "My celebrity," he said, "is a poor reflection of the values of today."[14]

Morality and Economics

Why, indeed, were Feuerstein's actions both so unusual and so widely heralded? Here is the paradox: On one hand, Feuerstein did not see his actions as extraordinary; he did what anyone would have done if they could. He felt he had acted with *common* decency. On the other hand, he was acclaimed because, even though most people agreed that he had done the right thing, his actions were perceived to be unusual. The public felt he had acted with *uncommon* decency, and lauded him as a hero and a saint. If everyone agrees that he did the right thing, why was it so unusual an action?

Other companies have not followed Feuerstein's example even though his actions garnered good publicity and may have even helped the company. Why don't others do the same? The answer is that most large companies are not privately owned by individuals like Feuerstein, but are publicly owned by shareholders. One might think that a publicly held company might have public obligations. The reality is that such companies are managed by professionals who are obligated under existing law to maximize returns to shareholders, whether or not this is in the greater public interest. Existing law not only does not encourage most employers to act as Feuerstein did, but may actually *prohibit* them from responding as he did. If the president of a publicly owned company had followed Feuerstein's example, he might have faced a lawsuit by disgruntled shareholders claiming that he was not maximizing the value of their shares and thus was acting in contradiction to his fiduciary duties to them as owners of the corporation.[15] Paying money to workers that the company had no legal duty to pay would take money out of the pockets of the shareholders. Feuerstein himself recognized this.[16] It is ironic that, under current law, privately held companies have greater freedom than publicly owned companies to develop business strategies that both keep the company profitable and protect the interests of employees and the community in which the business operates.

If what Feuerstein did was so admirable, why is it illegal for most business managers to do what he did? Let us put the question more broadly: Can a religious or moral person be successful in business? Is it possible to be good and to do well at the same time? Does morality require us to look out for each other? If so, why does the law get in the way?

The Feuerstein story is a symbol of the contradictions of our age. We are a nation seemingly committed to deregulation, the protection of private property, and the end of "welfare as we know it." At the same time, we are morally committed to the notions of equality, human dignity, compassion, and responsibility. These political and moral commitments are in some tension, if not outright contradiction. On one side are claims of property; on the other side are claims of humanity. On one side are claims to rights; on the other side are acknowledgments of responsibilities. On one side are the values of liberty and autonomy; on the other side are the values associated with security, social stability, and solidarity.

The Feuerstein story is fascinating because it demonstrates a deep ambivalence about our brave new world of relentless individualism. While many of us are attracted to the images of liberty embedded in the vision of limited government, we are also worried about the insecurity this entails. After all, liberty seems to mean freedom from obligation. The promotion of liberty is an invitation to act in a self-interested manner. Self-interest has a pleasant face; it means that we can live our lives on our own terms. But it also has a dark side; it promotes indifference to the effects of one's actions on others. Indifference to others is not a virtue.

When people go to church on Sunday or mosque or synagogue on Friday or Saturday, they hear about the sacredness of human life. They learn about obligations to others. They hear about the importance of charity. They reach out beyond themselves. They strive to give life meaning. But then they go to work on Monday and something dramatic happens. They set what they learned aside and compartmentalize, as if it only applied on the weekend or in the evenings. They forget what they heard about compassion and focus only on profit. They resist efforts to include safety features in cars. They seek relaxation of antipollution laws. They induce employees to work hard by false assurances of job security at the very moment they are making plans to close the factory. They vote for politicians who cut food stamps to poor children and deny government benefits to immigrants who are here legally.

This comparison is overblown and tendentious, to be sure. Self-interest has a legitimate and expansive role in both private and public life. In a pluralistic society that separates church and state, religious and moral ideals do not coincide exactly with the norms that govern our economic institutions, if only because different religious traditions have different views about the relevance of religion to economic life and the content of the relevant norms. At the same time, public norms underlying law and economics cannot be completely divorced from controversial norms about morality and social justice. The reaction to Feuerstein demonstrates a disconnect between widely shared moral intuitions and our prevalent economic institutions and norms. We value self-interest but we also value compassion, and the gap between our moral intuitions and our economic and political practices is particularly wide now. In an age that laments the loss of moral values and old-fashioned community life, it is jarring that public policy is so oriented to the virtues of liberty and self-reliance. Surely morality entails at least a mix of self-interest and altruism, if not a healthy dose of compassion.

We ignore our moral qualms about a market system that relentlessly casts individuals aside in the pursuit of short-run profits because we have been led to believe that regulation of the market infringes on both liberty and prosperity. The attractions of the model of limited government intervention in the world of the market are obvious, but the dangers are equally apparent. Freedom from overbearing government regulation is popular because it seems to promote both individual liberty and economic prosperity. But unrestrained markets can fail. Economists may wax eloquent about the magic of markets, but we did suffer a Great Depression when unregulated and speculative markets collapsed. And the benefits of markets may be distributed quite unequally. Our current era is one of economic growth combined with increasing inequality of both income and wealth. Moreover, prosperity is combined with instability and insecurity. In the age of global competition, downsizing, and rapid capital movement, people increasingly feel that they are being treated like numbers on a balance sheet. They face what Roberto Unger has called the "savagery of impatient money." [17]

Those who are looking for work face even more serious problems. Some downsized workers readjust and find fulfilling new jobs. Others do not have the skills needed to compete in this technological age. And the poor who are being thrown off welfare face insurmountable odds. The costs of maintaining a family, including food, clothing, housing, medical care, child care, and transportation, are higher than the wages available in the marketplace under the current minimum wage. Rebecca Blank notes that "full-time year-round work at the minimum wage produces $8,500 in gross income, well below the $11,900 poverty line for a family of three or the $15,000 poverty line for a family of 4." [18] This gap is the difference between the ideal of personal responsibility and the reality of desperation. It is these vulnerabilities that raise fears in the hearts of both welfare recipients and workers.

These fears explain the positive public reaction to Feuerstein. In an age of increasing uncertainty, Feuerstein seemed a bright light. His actions exposed the worries just beneath the surface in this era of economic prosperity. But they also revealed a different moral world. Richard Sennett has perceived that in this time of downsizing, people have begun to feel that they do not matter. "People are treated as disposable."[19] Their own efforts may come to naught; they may be fired despite working hard and successfully. "The system," Sennett writes, "radiates indifference. It does so in terms of the outcomes of human striving, as in winner-take-all-markets, where there is little connection between risk and reward."[20] Feuerstein bucked this trend. He treated his employees as if they mattered, because they *in fact* mattered to him. In so doing, he publicly recognized the value of their humanity. They count. Feuerstein was commended not because he was a saint but because it was widely felt that he had done the right thing in a world where many people do not. He had treated the people with whom he did business as many people wish they would be treated – as they believe they deserve to be treated. The question is not why Feuerstein's actions were praiseworthy (they were, after all, just common decency), but why a chief executive officer of a publicly owned corporation would be discouraged, and possibly even forbidden, by law to do what Feuerstein did. Why does the law get in the way? And why is it thought to be impossible to institutionalize these norms in the business world even when the law does not get in the way?

Personal responsibility is the rule of the day, but Feuerstein's other-regarding acts brought tears to many eyes. He was an owner entitled – by law – to consider his interests alone; but he was also a religious Jew who understood law differently. He felt obligated to act *lifnim mishurat hadin* – beyond the letter of the law. The larger community found this praiseworthy. When people do more than they are required to do by law, it sometimes means that they are unusually good. But sometimes, it means that the law is in need of change. Feuerstein's actions were like a mirror that forced us to look at ourselves and to consider what we really value. Companies may be managed for profit, but we also know that they may be the backbone of a local community. Deregulation is our new civil religion, but we are uncomfortable with the plant closings, downsizings, and indifference that accompany it. We value liberty but we recognize that it undermines security. Feuerstein was met with affection and gratitude because his actions suggested that it was possible to bridge the tensions we face between liberty and security, rights and responsibilities, property and humanity.

Progressive Strategies and Moral Suasion

A number of progressive scholars have recently argued for public policies to improve the condition of both working people and the non-working poor. They argue that realistic opportunities do not now exist to enable every person to enter the economic system on fair terms. This is partly the result of government policy, they claim, and they urge government action to remedy this problem. They have noted the disappearance of good jobs at good wages (James K. Galbraith, Katherine Newman, John Schwarz, William Julius Wilson); the impossible dilemmas of poor mothers in caring for their children and meeting demands to work at low-paid jobs without adequate transportation, child care, medical insurance, or housing (Mary Jo Bane, Rebecca Blank, Lisa Dodd, David Ellwood, Joel F. Handler and Yeheskel Hasenfeld, Gwendolyn Mink, Robert M. Solow); the increasing inequality of income and wealth (Galbraith, Edward Wolff); widening racial divides (Wilson, Mink, Douglas Massey, Nancy Denton, Cornel West); institutional stagnation (Roberto Mangabeira Unger and West); and unchecked corporate power (Charles Derber).[21]

These scholars have proposed a variety of strategies for redressing inequality and restoring the American dream to millions of Americans who find themselves outside the boundaries of prosperity at the beginning of the new century. They present a compelling picture of an economy and a politics gone wrong. They also offer a sense that something can, in fact, be done about it.[22] They point out that formulating policies that will work to restore access to the American dream for every person is a complicated business. Each solution creates its own problems and some solutions work at cross-purposes. Yet it is clearly possible to do better than we are currently doing to spread the benefits of economic life more evenly. We will accomplish this only if we wish it to be done. We will collectively wish it to be done only if we can build political support for appropriate governmental action. And we will build such support only if we can build a compelling *moral* case for doing something.

Economic policies get translated into law only when public support can be galvanized. And public support is galvanized most effectively when private interests appear to converge with public norms. People want public policies that further their interests, but they would like to believe that such policies will not be unfair to others. More often than not, new public policies are supported by arguments that affirm their fairness and justice, as well as their efficacy at protecting and promoting legitimate interests. The rhetoric of morality pervades our political system. The statute that ended "welfare as we knew it" was called the Personal Responsibility and Work Opportunity Reconciliation Act. Its supporters argued that it would leave welfare recipients better off and that it would both induce them to take personal responsibility and promote opportunities for work that had previously been denied to them.

The progressive scholars who have proposed new policies to create real opportunities for those set adrift by the end of welfare do not address the reasons why we lack the political will to do what they urge. They do not confront the ambivalence we feel about collective action to remedy the problems they identify. Nor do they confront the philosophic and legal barriers to doing what they so passionately claim is right. Why is there no movement to institutionalize Feuerstein's responses in policy or law so that other workers and other communities facing similar problems will find similar support? The problem is not that Americans lack compassion, but that American public policy does. Our political rhetoric is more individualist than our people are.

We have come to believe that actions by either government or business to remedy the problems of poverty or joblessness are in conflict with both legal principles and economic realities. Regulation of business seems to contradict hallowed principles of liberty and private property and established economic wisdom. People have a mistaken view that acting collectively on our compassionate impulses will undermine our legal and economic system at the core – that it will kill the goose that laid the golden egg.

No laws of economics or core principles of law prevent us from acting on individual and societal moral obligations to act compassionately to aid those victimized by economic change. It is widely assumed that property law protects the rights of owners to do what they like with their property and that these rights have few, if any limits. This view does not accord with the facts. There is far more continuity between our moral obligations and our legal institutions than most people realize. Although they are not identical, morality and law are not two completely separate systems of value. Rather, our core rules of property law contain multiple duties to limit property use so that it will not impinge on the legitimate interests of others. It will not undermine either private property or free enterprise to institutionalize through law the elements of Feuerstein's actions that seemed so strikingly admirable to many people. Indeed, establishing those elements as part of the law may not only *not* hurt our economic system but may well enhance it, as well as being the right thing to do.

Property and Obligation

Property is at the heart of the American self-image. With the collapse of communism, it is widely believed that an economic system that protects property rights not only produces the greatest prosperity but is an essential ingredient in creating a free and democratic society.[23] I believe it is right to say that property is related to freedom. But it is often wrongly thought that this means that both freedom and security are best enhanced by letting owners and businesses use their property as they please, without regulation or limitation and that no social or political supports are necessary to ensure that individuals can become owners. The truth of the matter is that property systems will self-destruct without regulations designed to ensure that owners do not use their property in ways inimical to others. Moreover, no one acquires property by their own efforts alone. Both governmental and nongovernmental support are essential to any system of property – at least one supported by law rather than by brute force.

Property promotes liberty by giving individuals the resources they need to create a home, engage in work, develop relationships with others, and live their lives on their own terms. If property is related to liberty, as I believe, then those who cannot obtain property cannot obtain liberty. Because property is exclusionary, protection of the rights of owners may have the effect of leaving others out of the system. It is not an accident that the crime rate has soared in South Africa, where roughly 10 percent of the people own 80 percent of the land as a result of the legacy of apartheid laws that denied the bulk of the population the right to own property simply because of their race.[24] Unless the government there can implement policies that spread access to property more widely, the newfound ideals of equality, liberty, and democracy will be fatally undermined. It is essential to shape our property institutions so that it is realistically possible for everyone to enter the system and obtain a decent livelihood.

CHAPTER TWO

Outside the Boundaries

The liberal views of Robert Montgomery, professor of economics at the University of Texas, made him unpopular with the Texas legislature. An investigation was set in motion. When he was asked if he favored private property, Montgomery replied, "I do — so strongly that I want everyone in Texas to have some."[1]

— John Kenneth Galbraith

The individual human [is] an inherently social being, inevitably dependent on others not only to thrive but even just to survive. This irreducible interdependency means that individuals owe one another obligations, not by virtue of consent alone but as an inherent incident of the human condition.[2]

— Gregory S. Alexander,
Commodity and Propriety

In the late nineteenth century, the Pullman's Palace-Car Company built a company town "where the streets, alleys, school houses, business houses, sewerage system, hotels, churches, theaters, waterworks, market places, dwellings, and tenements" were its "exclusive property." The attorney general of the state of Illinois sued the company, claiming that the establishment of a company town was illegal because it exceeded the powers granted the company in its corporate charter. The lower court ruled in favor of the company, but in 1898, the Illinois Supreme Court reversed the decision, ordering Pullman Village to be sold off. The court explained that a company town is "incompatible with the theory and spirit of our institutions."[3] Concentrated ownership is one form of property, but it is not a defensible form, and it is not the American way.

This view may be surprising. After all, we live in the midst of substantial, and growing, inequality of both wealth and income.[4] The institution of property itself seems to entail acceptance of the inevitability of inequality. As the U.S. Supreme Court stated in 1915, "since it is self-evident that . . . some persons must have more property than others, it is from the nature of things impossible to uphold freedom of contract and the right of private property without at the same time recognizing as legitimate those inequalities of fortune that are the necessary result of the exercise of those rights."[5]

It is true that a property system could not function if absolute equality needed to be maintained at every moment. But it is a logical error to conclude that the existence of *some* inequalities justify the existence of *any amount* of inequality. Nor does the inevitability of some inequality mean that all *forms* of property ownership are equally justified or equally conducive to promoting liberty, justice, social welfare, or material wealth. As the *Pullman* case illustrates, U.S. law has long taken into account the need to limit owners' rights in order to promote dispersal of ownership and to shape the contours of defensible social and political relationships.

The *Pullman* case illustrates a number of important points. First, property is a system as well as an individual entitlement. The character of the social relationships shaped by the property system is of paramount importance. Second, the property system favored in U.S. history is one that promotes the dispersal of ownership. This does not mean that the law prohibits the accumulation of great wealth. It means that the American dream includes the idea that anyone can make it; he or she can work hard, obtain property, especially a home. Third, property law establishes a compromise between the desire for change and the desire for stability. Finally, the law – including the law defining and regulating market relationships – promotes a variety of human values and not just the value of profit maximization. The question is not just whether a given legal rule makes us better off in terms of material wealth but whether it helps shape a world we want to inhabit. We need to know whether a particular rule or institution makes this a better place to live. Let me spin out the implications of each of these insights.

Property and Social Relations

Property law is a system, and not just a source of individual entitlement. Property systems not only grant ownership rights to individuals but regulate the relationships among those rights holders. The exercise of rights by one affects others. For this reason, the system of legal rights must be shaped to create an environment that will allow individuals both to obtain access to property and to enjoy their legal rights without unreasonable interference by others. This means that the rights of each must be curtailed to ensure an environment that allows all others to exercise their rights fully. Rights must be limited to protect rights.

This paradox arises because we do not live alone. The law – including the law of property – recognizes that our fate is tied to the fate of others. Moreover, the law does not exist only to protect our interests; it exists also to promote liberty and justice. These goals cannot be realized unless we act in ways that respect the interests of others, as well as ourselves. For this reason, the core precepts of property law require owners to use their property in a manner that is consistent with the legitimate interests of others. These other-regarding obligations suggest that our moral obligations and our legal institutions are more closely related than one might think. The law is highly protective of the prerogatives of owners, but it also recognizes that ownership may impose vulnerabilities on others and limits the rights of owners when their actions impinge on the legitimate interests of others.

The essence of property is the use of state power to assign ownership rights which grant owners both the freedom to use their property and the right to exclude others from it. The liberties of owners are associated with duties on nonowners to respect the legal rights of owners. The protection of owners secures a realm of stability for owners and for the community as a whole. It does this by limiting the freedom of nonowners in order to ensure security for owners. At the same time, these limits on freedom enlarge the owner's liberty by creating a space where the owner may act.

This principle of limiting freedom to promote security applies to owners, not only to non-owners. That is, owners cannot use their property to interfere with the reasonable expectations of other owners; nor can owners use their powers to prevent nonowners from becoming owners. If security is a goal of property, then this goal cannot be reserved for owners alone; it must extend to nonowners as well. For this reason, the law of property both protects the interests of established owners and ensures that conditions exist under which nonowners can obtain access to property and become owners themselves. Property thus promotes both access to ownership and stability for existing owners. Of course, these protections coexist with interests in freedom and liberty. Freedom and security interests are in tension with each other. Property law mediates between liberty and security, stability and change, the accumulation of wealth and the preservation of equality. Ownership may give security to the owner but it imposes a vulnerability on the nonowner. The question is what the distribution of security and vulnerability should be.

When we recognize property as a system, we see that what matters is not just the granting of ownership rights to individuals or the number of owners, but the *character of the social relationships* shaped by the property rights system. "Every law and every political choice," writes Jedediah Purdy, "is in part a judgment about the sort of country we will inhabit and the sorts of lives we will lead."[6] After all, slavery is a property system, although a horribly unjust one. Similarly, the company town is a possible property system, but it is not ours. Slavery is evil for obvious reasons. It treats people as if they were animals or machines; it assaults the dignity of the individual person while authorizing a form of tyranny by one group over another. The company town is also objectionable, and for surprisingly similar reasons. The company town concentrates too much power in the hands of a single owner; it also creates an indefensible form of social life.[7] The company town warps social and political relationships by denying citizens the material bases for independence and autonomy, as well as the institutions necessary for self-government.

The company town looks a little too much like aristocracy or feudalism. The company takes on the role of a lord, demanding service in return for access to land. Rather than allowing relationships between independent citizens with equal rights, the system creates one-sided relationships, with too much power concentrated in the owner. The dangers of such a power imbalance are evident. Such a property system affects social and political life in the community. In a recent example, a coal worker named Danny Fout lived in an apartment owned by his employer in West Virginia. When he joined the union in going on strike, as he was legally entitled to do, the employer responded by sending him an eviction notice – an action obviously designed to retaliate against him for striking and to discourage other workers from striking in the future. [8] A company that owned the entire town would have even more power than this employer did. [9]

Modern property law in the United States developed out of English property law. English property law reacted against the feudal arrangement of property in which the king handed out the land to a number of vassals in return for their services in defending his power and his realm. Those vassals, in turn, created personal arrangements with subvassals to perform those and other services. Eventually, almost everyone occupied a place in an elaborate feudal hierarchy, was tied to land, and was obligated to serve a lord who might serve a lord above him. The local lord served not only as the landowner but also as the local political authority, passing laws and holding court.

Over time, the law limited the powers of the lords and the sublords, pushing power downwards to those who worked the land. The property system developed fundamental legal principles designed to prevent the re-emergence of feudalism. It did so by technical rules of law that attempt to concentrate power in the hands of the vassals who were in actual possession of the land.

These rules were adopted in the United States. For example, in the early Republic, much of upper New York State was owned by a single landowner, Stephen Van Rensselaer, who "sold" property to tenant farmers on condition that they make yearly payments called "quit-rents" and that they pay one-quarter of the purchase price to him whenever they sold the land. Although the New York courts upheld the yearly rental obligations, they struck down the requirement that tenants pay a quarter of any sale proceeds to Van Rensselaer. In ruling on the legality of the property arrangements, the New York Court of Appeals recognized that feudal arrangements were prohibited in the United States. As in the *Pullman* case, the court wrestled with the question of whether the property rights created by Van Rensselaer were compatible with American institutions and traditions, specifically, the laws prohibiting feudal property relationships. [10]

Concentrated power and wealth in an overlord seemed to contradict the emerging norms associated with a republic of independent, equal citizens, with no formal differences of status or special rights related to hierarchical powers over land. The transfer tax struck down by the New York courts not only came too close to the kinds of feudal services that had been abolished in the United States, but substantially interfered with the ability of individual owners to buy and sell land. The rental payment however, seemed closer to what were perceived as legitimate landlord-tenant relationships compatible with a modern property system. Whatever the merits of the court's decision, it is important to recognize that the underlying question was whether the property arrangements were compatible with the traditions and norms of a free and democratic society. Those norms were hostile to property arrangements that concentrated power too heavily in the hands of a lord.

This is not to say that the American system limited the ability to accumulate wealth or was completely opposed to hierarchy or inequality. Indeed, the New York courts upheld the quitrent arrangements, even though they were so unpopular that they eventually led to widespread civil disobedience and unrest. More fundamentally, most people were either left out of the property system entirely or relegated to inferior status within it. Those excluded from full rights were white women and African Americans and American Indians, both male and female. Status relationships existed between masters and servants, as well as between husbands and wives.

Race has obviously played a major role in the development of American property law. The preservation of slavery as an institution at the Constitutional Convention represented a particularly unfortunate compromise on the fundamental values of a new nation dedicated to the notions of both liberty and democracy. It cannot be said, however, that the institution of slavery was inconsistent with the institution of property; slavery is, after all, a form of property and protection for property was one of the major goals of the Constitution. It is, however, an *unacceptable* form of property – one that contradicts other values we hold dear. Similarly, the Jim Crow laws that authorized and later imposed the "separate but equal" requirement on public accommodations constructed access to property in a manner that we now view as anathema. Not until the 1960s were laws passed that began an effective assault on social practices that excluded individuals from ownership based on race in many parts of the United States.

The abolition of feudalism, aristocracy, and racial caste have implications for the law of property. Both particular legal rules and targeted regulatory policies are necessary to ensure that the distribution and exercise of property rights are compatible with underlying norms of equality, autonomy, and social justice.

Another example occurs in the context of family property. In the early nineteenth century, substantial limits were placed on the power of married women to own and manage property in their own right.[11] Husbands were given extraordinary powers to manage property ostensibly owned by their spouses. These inequalities were substantially changed – although not eradicated – by the Married Women's Property Acts, passed in the late nineteenth century. At the same time, substantial inequalities remained between the property rights of men and women.[12] As late as 1970, some states still gave husbands management powers over jointly owned property of husbands and wives. It was only in 1981, in the case of *Kirchberg v. Feenstra,* that the Supreme Court finally declared these unequal management arrangements unconstitutional under the equal protection clause of the Fourteenth Amendment.[13]

All these examples demonstrate that property is a social institution and that the law regarding the prerogatives of owners has significant effects on the shape and character of social relationships and the life of the community. The establishment of a property system affects human relationships. It is imperative that the law of property take into account the effect of alternative constructions of property rights on those relationships.

Exclusion and Access

People tend to think that property rights protect those who are clever or fortunate enough to get property but that no one has any guarantee that they will be among those blessed with property. The institution of private property allows individuals to obtain property in a variety of ways, including by work, by gift, or by inheritance. People can keep what they get or can exchange it with others through sale or investment. They can exclude others from what they own or share what they have. This is all well understood and widely accepted. However, it is not well understood or widely accepted that property institutions implicate any entitlements to *have* property. The general view is that people who cannot get property in any of the approved ways are not entitled to own anything. In this view, property institutions create opportunities only; they do not guarantee outcomes. We are free to get property if we can but there is no assurance that we will. We are entitled to own what we can get, but the law does not ensure that each of us will become an owner.

This view is an inaccurate but familiar account of Anglo-American property law principles. Property systems define approved ways to get property and the scope of the rights of the owner. But they do more than this. They are structured to create conditions that will make it possible for ownership to be widely dispersed. The American system has always attempted to ensure that access to the property system is widely available. In fact, the law of property is a bridge between the haves and the have-nots.

The law protects nonowners in two different ways. First, it protects nonowners from oppression at the hands of owners. It does this by limiting what owners can do with their property. Second, the law fosters the conditions necessary for individuals to obtain access to the ownership system. Beyond this, it establishes ground rules that promote a tolerable degree of equality in distribution. This is not to say that the system performs these functions well. As Roberto Unger notes, our inherited property regime seems to "care more for the absoluteness of the property right than for the number of real economic agents with access to productive resources or for the range of ways in which they have access to it." [14] At the same time, the institution of private property presupposes a plurality of owners. Although at one time we excluded large segments of the population from the class of those entitled to the status of owner, our current practice is to universalize access.

The property system favored in U.S. history is one that promotes the dispersal of ownership. This dispersal of ownership allows a well-functioning competitive market to exist; disperses power; grants widely the benefits of independence, stability, and liberty that are associated with property ownership; and promotes access to the means necessary for a dignified human life. To achieve these goals, the legal system regulates the manner in which individuals create and obtain property rights, as well as the ways in which they use them.

The distribution of property is determined for the most part by market exchanges and gifts (especially inheritance), but those exchanges are shaped, conditioned, and regulated by social norms and law. The law, especially the law of property, has a huge effect on the distribution of access to the valued things of the world. The dilemma of distribution arises because owners are generally entitled to exclude nonowners from their property. The law, however, contains numerous rules designed to ensure that access to property is available to everyone. And our political history is replete with government action, such as the homestead laws, designed to ensure widespread dispersal of ownership. This latter principle has sometimes been sacrificed to the former, but it has never been relinquished entirely.

Property concerns things needed for human life. At the most elemental level, property gives us a place to be: a place to live, a place to work.[15] It gives us the means to thrive: food to eat, clothing to wear. It gives us things that make life enjoyable, meaningful, and fun. But property does not only provide our material needs. It enables us to exercise autonomy, to enjoy our liberties, to shape our destiny, to form relationships with others, to live a human life. We cannot live our lives without the means to do so.

Property is essential to human liberty. This observation is commonplace. It is usually taken to mean that government actions that interfere with the rights of owners are inherently suspect. Laws limiting what owners can do with their property seem, on these grounds, to interfere with liberty. Something is missing in this conventional interpretation of the relation between property and liberty. Liberty is promoted not only by allowing owners to do what they like with what they own; liberty is promoted by ensuring that everyone can become an owner.

We protect property rights because control of property helps individuals to live a fully human life. Access to material resources is a precondition, not only of subsistence, but of the capacity to shape one's life, to create a home, to develop relationships with others, and to engage in meaningful work. Access to property promotes security by ensuring stable control over the resources needed for a dignified life. If the ability to lead a decent life is important, it is equally important for every person. If property is necessary to obtain the ability to lead a decent life, then, every person must have a realistic opportunity to obtain access to property.

As Jeremy Waldron explains, "People need private property for the development and exercise of their liberty; that is why it is wrong to take all of a person's private property away from him, and that is why it is wrong that some individuals should have had no private property at all." Since each person is entitled to be treated as equally important, a legitimate property system must ensure that access to a minimum amount of property is available *for every single person*. This does not mean that property must be equally distributed. It does mean that,

taken as a whole, the legal system may not have the effect of denying individuals the effective ability to obtain entry into the system.
"There is no adequate right-based argument to be found which provides an adequate justification for a society in which some people have
lots of property and many have next to none."[16] We are each entitled
to the means necessary for a dignified human life. This means that we
should each be legally entitled to ownership of some property and to
a realistic opportunity to work.

Ensuring that each person has access to property requires the legal
system to be structured so as to prevent the exclusion of individuals from the system. If property is essential to a human life, those who
are outside the boundaries of property must be allowed in. But property itself entails the legal right to exclude others. We have a paradox.
Laura Underkuffler-Freund explains that property rights are unique
because they concern things needed for human life and because the
granting of a property right to one person simultaneously denies that
right to others.[17] If property gives the owner the right to control resources needed for human life – and to exclude others from those essential resources – then it is possible that the protection of property
will have the effect of denying property rights to those outside the system. In order to ensure that things necessary to human life are available to everyone, the property rights of all must be structured so that
all can come inside the boundaries of the system and acquire property.
It may be necessary to limit property – even to tax owners – to ensure
that fair access to property is available to everyone. It may be necessary
to regulate property rights to protect property rights.

Before the 1960s, an African-American family traveling in the
South would have had a lot of trouble. They would have had difficulty
finding a restaurant where they could eat or a motel where they could
sleep. They would have had to plan way ahead, pack food with them,
sleep at friends' homes, or sleep in their car. Owners had legally protected rights to exclude on the basis of race not only those seeking a
night's rest or a meal, but those seeking to buy property themselves.
After valiant struggles, led by ordinary and extraordinary people, this
nation concluded that race-based exclusion from lunch counters, mo-

tels, and the ranks of home owner could not stand in a nation committed to equal protection of the law.

This is why property rights cannot be absolute. The granting of a property right does not concern the owner alone. Because owners generally have the legal right to exclude nonowners, the granting of a property right to one person *simultaneously denies that right to others*.[18] If property concerns things necessary for human life and property rights give owners the legal right to deny those things to others, then the exercise of property rights may allow some people to exclude others from the things necessary to human life. John Locke long ago recognized that property could not be justified as a social institution if some were able to monopolize ownership of goods needed for human life. Ownership is justified only "where there is enough and as good left in common for others.[19] Since the right to exclude necessarily affects others, a system that is true to the norms underlying the institution of private property cannot allow some to monopolize access to property.

Nor can access to public places, such as sidewalks and public squares and parks, be denied on an arbitrary basis. The Supreme Court recently struck down Chicago's antiloitering ordinance.[20] Although designed to combat gangs, it was drafted in a way that allowed the use of racial criteria to prevent youths from hanging out in public in groups. The ordinance gave too much discretion to the police. Worse still, it effectively made access to public places partially contingent on race. The ordinance made police officers disperse individuals who the officers "reasonably believed" were "criminal street gang members." Police may use race as a proxy for determining who they think is a gang member. Without constitutionally adequate controls, this kind of ordinance could wrongfully exclude individuals from public places on the basis of race or ethnicity.

A recent lawsuit in Miami challenged the police practice of arresting homeless people for sleeping and urinating in public. The judge found that there were not enough shelters in the city to house the number of people who were without places to sleep. Because of this, the judge ordered the police not to arrest homeless people sleeping at a public park.[21] Jeremy Waldron explains that "everything that is done has to be done somewhere. No one is free to perform an action unless there is somewhere he is free to perform it."[22] The normal operation of property law entitles owners to prevent homeless persons from sleeping on their property. The effect of the universal assignment of ownership rights in land is to deny homeless persons a place where they are legally entitled to sleep. And unless it is constitutionally permissible to outlaw sleep, it must be unconstitutional to deny a person the legal right sleep *somewhere*.

Stability and Change

Property law establishes a compromise between the desire for change and the desire for stability. The very institution of property might be understood as created to ensure stability for the owner – freedom from worry that what one claims as one's own property will be taken by force. At the same time, the free use of property is destabilizing. Competition creates losers as well as winners. Economic uses of property are not static but dynamic, and the market itself generates new businesses while creating bankruptcies.

At the end of the twentieth century, we have come to celebrate flexibility, movement, innovation, retooling, reorganization, mergers, and retraining. We now expect employees to shift jobs several times, even many times, during their lives. Business owners also face global competition. This new world creates problems. Richard Sennett argues that in our economic system "people are treated as disposable" within a regime that "radiates indifference." These practices "obviously and brutally diminish the sense of mattering as a person, of being necessary to others."[23] This has devastating personal and social consequences.

The disposable employee faces the further problem of a marked increase in inequality of both wealth and income. This inequality is partially caused and certainly exacerbated by the fact that many of the new jobs that are replacing old jobs offer very low wages. John Schwarz measured the wages one would have to obtain to live a decent human life in our society. It turns out that the minimum wage does not come close to this level. He then measured the number of "good jobs" – those paying a minimally decent wage – and compared it to the number of people searching for jobs or who are currently in jobs that do not pay good wages. There is a substantial shortfall – almost 16 million jobs short.[24] The number of people demanding good jobs is greater than the available number of those jobs. Now one might presume that the economy will adjust. But it might not. Economist James K. Galbraith is convinced it will not adjust (or will not adjust fast enough to protect those who are vulnerable) without a change in government policy.[25]

One day, during my college economics class, Professor Randall Bartlett asked us if we thought economic competition was a good idea. We all said yes, that competition gave consumers choices and encouraged companies to produce what people wanted and needed at the lowest cost. I recall that he answered, "Suppose you never knew, when you came to class, whether there might be someone already sitting in your seat – ready, willing, and able to do a better job than you. You would never know, day to day, whether you retained a place here at the college. Would you like that?" His question made us recognize the boundaries of competition that we assumed and cherished – the boundaries set by settled expectations. What we in fact cherished was the security of knowing that we had a continuing relationship with the school, that we had time – over the course of the semester, the school year, the four-year program – to develop our skills, to learn, to perform, to demonstrate our knowledge.

What we valued was property. By paying tuition – with cash, scholarships, and loans – we had an expectation of continued access to our place in the college, an expectation that gave us the freedom to learn. We had security: the knowledge that if we worked hard, and did what was expected of us, we would be able to reap what we had sowed. This, after all, is the basis of the modern idea of property. If there were no protection for property, one might hesitate to plant a crop if someone else could simply swoop in at the last minute and seize it. "In such condition," argued Thomas Hobbes, "there is no place for Industry; because the fruit thereof is uncertain; and consequently no Culture of the Earth."[26] On this point, at least, John Locke agreed with Hobbes that the absence of law would mean that "the enjoyment of [property] is very uncertain and constantly exposed to the invasion of others." Creating a state to enforce property rights frees us from a condition that is "full of fears and continual dangers."[27] Property affords security. Providing this security is the job of government. Property rights do not entail freedom from government regulation; they derive their meaning from the fact that owners are entitled to call on the state to enforce their ability to control the resources they own. Determining the circumstances under which we are so entitled is the job of the law.

Property law creates stability by limiting liberty in order to promote security. It does so by delegating state power to owners to enforce their legitimate claims to security. It is wrong to identify property with a situation of deregulation. Property is about government protection. Property law mediates between conflicting claims of liberty and security. The property system cannot legitimately be structured so as to exclude individuals from access to the means necessary to a dignified human life. The laws and policies governing and surrounding property must protect established claims while simultaneously ensuring the presence of realistic opportunities for those who have not yet been able to establish property claims.

Professor Bartlett's image of daily competition for seats at the college was meant to be understood as a nightmare. But, as Robert Kuttner points out, reality is coming closer and closer to such a vision.[28] The new practices of downsizing, outsourcing, and hiring temporary and contingent labor make more of us vulnerable to day-to-day competition. This may increase flexibility, but it also leaves families and communities without stable moorings. The free movement of capital searching for the highest profit – and no other goal – destabilizes our communities. It used to be believed that labor was more mobile than capital. It was thought that a factory could not easily be moved from one location to another while people could move or even emigrate. Whether or not this supposition was ever true, the situation today is almost the reverse: capital today appears incredibly mobile. If you don't like the tax policy of one state, move to another. If you face a unionized workforce accustomed to high wages, shut down and move somewhere where unions are anathema and the standard of living allows payment of low wages. While capital is mobile, labor appears relatively less so. Although people still move around a lot and may do so to find employment, the impediments to movements of people today seem greater than the impediments to movement of capital. And of course immigration controls force most people to stay put.

The movement of capital – with layoffs, massive plant closings, and relocations of corporate operations – has serious effects on the communities left behind. Of course, movement may benefit the communities that attract investment and new investors may move into the old community. But it is still the case that our new age of flexible capitalism disrupts lives. A certain amount of stability is essential for a strong community, and rapid movement of business can undermine that stability. There is a contradiction between conservative calls to reestablish traditional values with a strong moral framework for individual and community life and the simultaneous demand to deregulate the economy, which promotes the destabilization of existing business ventures by the rapid movement of capital all over the world.

We need economic growth, but we also need strong communities. Change and flexibility are wonderful when they express and serve the liberty we cherish. But we also value stability, especially social stability. I have noted that the institution of property is premised on the need for stability; legal protection for owners is what gives them the security of knowing that they will be able to manage what they own and thus will be able to manage their lives. They have justified expectations and the law will protect those. At the same time, the exercise of property rights affects others and the march of global competition produces losers, as well as winners. The institution of property was created to manage the tension between stability and change and between liberty and security. This means that we have hard questions to ask about the distribution of vulnerability and prosperity.

This does not mean that we should be nostalgic about the old form of capitalism. It does mean that it is incumbent on us to determine what the necessary correlatives to stable communities are today. If lifetime careers are no longer going to be the norm, then we need to determine how people are going to establish the kind of environment needed for secure family life. One might want, for example, to ensure the portability of pensions and to promote the continuity of health insurance. Freedom to acquire and use property – and to assist in its creation – depend on public and private investments in education and training for new and emerging jobs, as well as investment in job-creating businesses in areas hard hit by economic disruptions. If we want people to form strong attachments to their communities, we need jobs where people live.

Yet we face resistance to public policy and law designed to ameliorate the situation of those who are cast aside in the economy's acts of "creative destruction." In recent years, the personal responsibility mantra has been used to attack welfare. Public assistance is said to be incompatible with incentives to accept personal responsibility for one's own fate. We constantly hear criticism of those who demand rights but seem unwilling to accept responsibilities. We urge welfare mothers to accept responsibility for their own lives and stop demanding so many rights. At the same time, we hear calls to deregulate property owners. Now one might view these messages as consistent; after all, they both suggest that one should rely on oneself alone. But they are fundamentally inconsistent in one basic respect. The push to deregulate suggests that the one group entitled to rights without responsibilities is the group composed of owners of property. They seem to be entitled to the protection of their rights without any correlative responsibilities. This view might make sense if the exercise of a property right were self-regarding – if it concerned the owner alone. But the exercise of a property right is anything but self-regarding. The use of property affects others as well as oneself, and the exercise of the right to exclude necessarily places obligations on others – obligations that may exclude them from access to the means of earning a living. Personal responsibility does not only mean the duty to take care of oneself. It also means the duty to act so that one's actions do not unduly interfere with the ability of others to obtain similar ends.

The conventional view interprets property and contract as embodiments of laissez-faire. Within this analysis, the law assigns *ownership* rights by reference to individual actions of possession and labor, and owners are entitled to control their property and to exchange it with others. When owners engage in contractual relations – exchanging goods or labor – they are free to make whatever agreements they wish without oppressive government interference. In this view, the basic contractual principle is one of *freedom of contract*.

This laissez-faire ideology was never implemented in its entirety. The conception of property suggested by the laissez-faire theory is a mirage. There has never been a time when owners in a democratic market economy were allowed to do whatever they wanted with their property. Uses of property must be regulated to ensure that owners do not interfere with other legitimate, legally protected interests. Both policy and law promote widespread access to the property system, and this may require limiting both property uses and transactions.

The laissez-faire conception of contract is no closer to the mark. It has never been the case in the United States that contractual relations were completely free of regulation. The law of contract does not allow individuals to bargain for whatever terms they like. We have a host of consumer protection regulations designed to ensure that justified expectations are protected in market exchanges. Our securities laws not only prohibit companies from lying to investors; they also require companies to reveal material information that prospective stockholders would want to know in deciding whether to buy a company's stock. Failure to disclose such information is a form of fraud subject to heavy penalties; it is seen as a kind of theft of the investor's money.[29]

Kent Greenfield has pointed out that we are inconsistent in our willingness to protect market actors from the vicissitudes of hard dealing. Our securities laws provide extraordinary protection for investors, but we do not provide similar protections for employees. They are left vulnerable even to false and misleading statements by employers. Employers have been allowed to induce employees to work hard with assurances that if they do so, they will continue to have jobs, and then to renege on those assurances by closing the factory in question or by moving it to another location. In such cases, the courts find that the employer not only did not commit fraud but that the employees have no claim for breach of contract. Employer assurances are not sufficiently definite to constitute actual promises. Unless the employer uttered the words "I promise," the courts find the employer's statements all unenforceable puffery.[30]

Why is it that the protections extended to shareholders are not extended to workers? In this context, there is widespread opposition to "regulation" of the market. But when similar protections are granted to investors, they are somehow not seen as oppressive regulations; indeed, such protections are justified by the policy of preventing fraud — a policy understood as preventing a form of theft. Regulation sometimes wrongly interferes with legitimate interests in freely controlling property and bargaining for terms one wants, but often it is in place precisely because it protects, rather than interferes with, justified expectations. We are not entirely consistent in our policies, however, and it is apparent that those who are most vulnerable sometimes receive the least amount of protection.

Property is a system of regulated relationships. It is the job of the law to manage tensions between competing interests in access and exclusion, change and stability, wealth and equality, liberty and security. The question for us is: what values should inform us as we choose property rules and institutions? How should the law shape economic and social life? One possibility is to ignore distributive issues and simply try to maximize the size of the economic pie. From reading the papers, one would think that this was our national goal. By all accounts, the country seems to be doing well. We read little in the papers about those who are struggling, those who are not making it, those who have slipped through the cracks.

There is another possibility. We could pay attention to those on the margins, those outside the boundaries. We could adjudicate the tensions we face between competing interests by developing laws and policies that will spread the wealth more evenly and allow every person to obtain a decent life. The crucial question is: Why should we do this? Why should we worry about those who are most vulnerable? Why should we care that 20 percent of our children are living in dire poverty? We could focus on the importance of human dignity, the sanctity of the individual, the nostrum that no one is an island. I believe we have even deeper reasons. That is the subject of the next chapter.

CHAPTER THREE

The Edges of the Field

Now when your brother sinks down (in poverty)
and his hand falters beside you,
then shall you strengthen him
as (though) a sojourner and resident-settler,
and he is to live beside you.[1]

— Lev. (*Vayikra*) 25:35

The one who says, What is mine is mine and what is yours is
yours, is middling [neither a saint nor wicked]. Some say this
is the mark of the people of Sodom.[2]

— *Pirkei Avot* (Ethics of the Fathers),

perek 5 mishnah 13

Two weeks before Christmas Day in 1997, a homeless man named José Flores went to sleep on the Boston Common. It was a cold night and he did not survive. "Curled for sleep and solace on the chilled earth of a world-famous public park," reflected Patricia Smith, "José Flores died of being alone, and the wind was a blanket laid over him."[3] We do not know exactly why he slept outside. We know that he was an alcoholic. Since no alcohol is allowed in shelters, alcoholics who spend the night in shelters go into temporary withdrawal. He may have chosen to sleep outside for this reason.[4] Perhaps he could have found a safe place to sleep if only he had tried harder. Beds were available at the Pine Street Inn shelter in Boston and Flores knew how to get there. Perhaps he should have had the strength to go without alcohol for the night. He had done this before.[5] But one thing is certain. People do not voluntarily sleep outdoors in wintertime if they have a family to be with or a safe place to go. Without property of his own, José Flores had no place to be.

The institution of private property may not be responsible for his death. After all, responsibility is a human matter. Flores had other choices. At the same time, his choices were not unconstrained; his illness substantially contributed to the circumstances leading to his death.[6] He needed help to deal with his illness, and had tried without success to get into treatment programs. He had also tried to find permanent housing. Nothing worked out.[7] Perhaps he should have been more persistent. Perhaps his condition and his frustration that his efforts had not paid off made it hard for him to be persistent. Perhaps he could have been saved if greater efforts – or different kinds of efforts – had been made to help him. Perhaps, in the end, nothing could have been done.

A little more than a year after the death of José Flores, two more homeless men died in similar circumstances in the city of Boston.[8] A total of eight homeless men died on the streets of Boston in the winter of 1999. Most had problems of addiction. None had access to shelter that would have kept him from freezing to death.

In December 1998, the first welfare recipients to reach the two-year limit established by the Commonwealth of Massachusetts were cut from the rolls. Some of them will adjust. Some will not. All will struggle to make ends meet, to take care of their children.

The problems of the mentally ill and alcoholic homeless population are complicated. Many refuse help. Still, I am haunted by this phrase: "He died of being alone." José Flores might not have died if he had somewhere he was welcome, someone who would take him in, on his own terms. "Home is where, when you have to go there,/ They have to take you in," Robert Frost told us, if we did not already know.[9] And if one has no family and no home, or if one has outworn one's welcome, what then? We all need places of our own or others to treat us as a members of the larger family, the human family, and to ensure that we have somewhere to be.

Yet, in these boom economic times, we have suppressed any sense of urgency about the fate of people who are being drowned by the rising tide and who find themselves in desperate circumstances. We seem to have convinced ourselves that they have only themselves to blame for their predicament. Or we have become overly skeptical of government and overly confident in the virtues of the "free market" and "personal responsibility." Those who favor government programs to aid the victims of economic change are derided as mushy headed and sentimental, "bleeding-heart" liberals who have no understanding of the ways of the world. It is an age of "tough love" – abandoning the vulnerable and justifying it as the ultimate demonstration of respect for individual dignity. This view enables us to suppress any sense that we have a moral duty to respond to the suffering of other human beings in our midst.

When we step into the church or the synagogue or the mosque, we hear a very different message. We are told to love our neighbors as ourselves. We are taught to be generous, understanding, compassionate. There but for the grace of God go we. Jews hear the words of the Torah: "Open your hand to the poor" (Deut. [*D'varim*] 15:11). "God upholds the cause of the orphan and the widow, and befriends the stranger, providing him with food and clothing. You too must befriend the stranger, for you were strangers in the land of Egypt" (Deut. [*D'varim*] 10:18–19). Christians hear these words and the words of Jesus: "For I was hungry and you gave me food, I was thirsty and you gave me drink. . . . As often as you did it for one of my least brothers, you did it for me" (Matt. 25:35–40). Moslems are told by the Qur'an: "As for the orphan, you shall not oppress him;/ And as for the beggar, you shall not drive him away" (*Al-Duha* 93:9–10).[10]

Those who are not religious also find occasion to be in touch with their ultimate values. At funerals, one does not generally hear praise for how much money someone made. One hears how good the deceased was to family and friends, how she or he treated others. They are remembered for the acts of kindness they performed. We often find that we praise individuals who care about others and who do not think about themselves alone. It is important to remember these feelings, these beliefs, these values when we think about politics, law, and economics. Our current political rhetoric has gone too far from our values of solidarity, caring, compassion, and kindness and too much in the direction of abandoning those left behind by the economy.

In the United States, property and religion are usually viewed as private matters – property because ownership is a bastion of autonomy against government power, and religion because conscience is protected from state establishment of religion. There are good reasons for protecting both individual autonomy and freedom of religion and conscience. These values are deeply embedded in our constitutional tradition. At the same time, morality cannot be entirely separated from either law or religion. And the law of property – the law governing the marketplace – depends on moral choices about the just contours of social life. Our views about minimum standards of decency and the requisites of an economic system compatible with human dignity are crucially influenced by the sources of our ultimate values and beliefs. The framers of the Constitution wanted to grant great protection for property, but they also wanted a nation with widespread ownership of property.[11] This idea of extending ownership to many, rather than limiting it to a feudal aristocracy or a nobility, was based partly on religious notions about the dignity of the individual. Moreover, the framers assumed that protection for property would coexist with religious practices that included obligations to others.

Given the ambiguities in the meaning of property, it is important to establish which values we will use to define the appropriate contours of legal rights. Those values determine the kinds of social relationships the law encourages and the kinds it precludes. Religion may provide insight. I examine religious rhetoric here partly in hopes of eliciting some recognition or evoking some persuasion through these traditions. But I also believe that we can learn from centuries of study and debate about the appropriate role of morality in the economic world. Major religions have grappled with the question of what obligations a good person has in the world of commerce, and have suggested ways to make an economic system compatible with the full range of our values. By looking at religious traditions, we may deepen our engagement with those values and find some inspiration on how to negotiate tensions we face between the pursuit of profit and the pursuit of humanity.

I will start with the tradition that motivated Feuerstein partly because it will help us understand how he conceptualized his role as an owner and partly because it is my tradition and I know it best. But there is another reason to begin here. The Jewish tradition is one source of modern conceptions of the importance of the individual, a belief that is central to our legal and philosophical tradition. The Bible teaches that each person was created in the image of God, and that what we do, each of us, matters. The sanctity of each person inevitably suggests that every human being, simply by virtue of her or his status as a human being, deserves a place in the world. For this reason, the Jewish tradition is highly protective of both private property and the poor and the oppressed. It therefore illustrates the possibility of recognizing strong moral obligations without undermining either the institution of property or economic prosperity. I will then move to Islam and Christianity to show that the obligations in Jewish law and ethics are neither unique nor outside the mainstream of religious belief in the United States.

The Flood

Property is granted enormous protection in the Jewish tradition. It forms two of the Ten Commandments: you shall not steal and you shall not covet your neighbor's belongings. Jewish law has devoted a significant amount of attention to defining the rights of owners. Several tractates of the Talmud deal with the rules concerning ownership of property. [12] Why is protection for property one of the central moral teachings in the *Tanakh* (the Jewish Bible) and especially in the Torah — the five books of Moses?

Remember the story of Noah and the Flood. The Torah says in Genesis (*Bereishit*) 6:11 that God destroyed the world because it was "corrupt" (*vatishakhet* ותשחת) and filled with *khamas* (חמס). The word *khamas* is variously translated as "violence," "lawlessness," "wrongdoing," or "outrage." [13] This wrongdoing was so horrible that

God "was sorry/that he had made humankind on earth,/and it pained his heart."[14] With all the evil doings one can observe in human history, what evil could be so terrible that it would make God regret having created human beings in the first place? What was so terrible that it "pain[ed] the heart of God"?

Rashi,[15] the great medieval commentator on the *Torah*, interprets the first reason for the destruction of the world – "corruption" – as "lewdness and idolatry."[16] Sexual sin and idolatry led to "indiscriminate punishment [which] kills innocent and guilty alike."[17] Rashi interprets these sins as having such drastic consequences as to bring a flood, a form of punishment that ignores justice, that punishes "good and bad" alike.[18] Avivah Gottlieb Zornberg suggests that "both sexual sins and idolatry may seem to be 'generous' sins. In them, human beings often experience and express a yearning to transcend the self, to relate to the other."[19] The ultimate cause of God's regret at creating humanity may lie in the second reason for the destruction of humanity: *khamas*. Rashi interprets *khamas* ("violence") as meaning "the sin of robbery." Other sages agree with him.[20] Tradition has it that sexual sin and idolatry were not enough to result in the Flood. Rashi writes that the "divine decree was sealed against them *only because of robbery*."[21] Although sexual sin and idolatry brought "total indiscriminate destruction" to the world, "it is only because of robbery, disrespect for private property, that the edicts are signed and sealed."[22] Why would Rashi identify robbery, the violent seizure of property, as the straw that broke the camel's back, the mark of a world that could not be redeemed?

The midrashic commentary (the commentary of the Jewish teachers) on the sexuality of the generation of the Flood emphasizes its "rapacious self-assertion."[23] "The divine beings saw how beautiful the daughters of men were and took wives from among those that pleased them" (Gen. [*Bereishit*] 6:2). They "took." Here is a clue to the relation between sexual sin and robbery; putting these two phenomena together suggests rape. This kind of sexuality is "not an act of love, but an act of robbery."

The essential paradigmatic act of sexual sin is thus an act of rapacious self-assertion, which sweeps away all other "worlds," all other selves. When Rashi says that the verdict against the Flood generation was sealed only because of the sin of *robbery,* we can understand him to be describing the *nature* of the prevailing sexual fantasy (and idolatrous fantasy) of the period. This is a fantasy in which self swells to fill all worlds, a colonial expansionism that radically denies the existence of other worlds of self and culture. "Either me or you. . . . " Essentially, this is a sexuality of cruelty, not of erotic relationship. It is a "pursuit of ecstasy which necessarily excludes attention to other people." At base it is, to use [Richard] Rorty's term, "a lack of curiosity." [24]

Robbery is used here as the mark of a lack of curiosity about the needs of the other. It is a willingness to take, and to take violently. It ignores the other as a human being, as a person created in the image of God. It aligns with idolatry in the sense that the robber assumes that he can act without being observed by the sleepless eyes of God and that the person who is being violated is not due the respect, the care, the dignity one would give a being through whose eyes the divine spark shines. It is idolatrous in the sense that the perpetrator worships something of his own creation – essentially worshiping himself – and thereby violates the boundaries of others.

Zornberg notes that after the Flood, Noah spends more than seven months shut up inside the ark. Why? Why does God make him spend this time shut up with his family and the animals? What is he doing? The rabbis say that Noah was learning the feeding schedules of the animals. [25] The feeding schedules of the animals? Why is this the important thing he must learn? What is going on?

Zornberg notes that when God tells Noah everyone will be swept away but him and his family, Noah does not question, he does not protest, he does not speak up for the innocent who will be destroyed along with the guilty. Some interpretations assume that Noah was the only righteous man in his generation, but Rashi, and other scholars, presume the opposite. The Flood sweeps away everything indiscriminately in its path, good and bad alike. When God tells Abraham the plan to destroy Sodom (*Sedom*) and Gomorrah (*Amorah*), Abraham protests and speaks up for the innocent who may suffer. Abraham represents a more developed state of moral consciousness, demonstrating concern for the other, while Noah is content if his family is saved. He does not speak up for others.

The experience in the ark, the long confinement, according to the rabbis, is a seminar in the moral consciousness that the generation of the Flood lacked: an ability to attend to the needs and realities of others. The "righteous" person is defined by the "capacity to nurture the needy." Learning to feed the animals what they need when they need it "becomes a year-long workshop in the kindness that [Richard] Rorty defined as 'curiosity.' " The "knowing of need is the highest measure of that curious, tender concern that characterizes God and God-like man."[26]

We have come full circle from robbery (protection for property) to kindness (attention to the needs of others). What is the message of the Flood story? Is it about protection of the rights of the owner or protection of the needy? The rabbinic interpretation unites these principles; it does not see them as contradictory. Robbery is inattention to the other, careless crossing of boundaries, but it is also a failure to give the other what is the other's due. Zornberg notes that the destruction of Sodom similarly revolved around the sins of rape and robbery. The sexual sin in Sodom is not sodomy, as is commonly believed, but rape, and it is seen by the rabbis as a particularly evil form of rape. It is the rape of strangers, travelers, visitors to Sodom. They are far from home, far from family, with no place to sleep except in the homes of strangers. They are peculiarly vulnerable. The robbery in Sodom involved a failure of hospitality to strangers and a lack of concern for the poor. The prophet Ezekiel identifies the sin of Sodom as "arrogance." "She and her daughters had plenty of bread and untroubled tranquillity; yet she did not support [literally, hold the hand] of the poor and the needy" (Ezek. 16:49). The midrash contains stories of travelers who are tricked, denied food, and left to die. They are robbed of life, of the sustenance they need, of the portion they are owed, of what they own. It "tells of a Sodomite custom to give the poor money marked with the sign of the giver. When the storekeepers refused to honor the currency, the poor died of starvation and the owner reclaimed his wealth."[27] They starved the stranger by withholding sustenance.

How does the obligation to take care of the traveler and the poor relate to robbery? From the common law viewpoint, it seems, they would be opposites. Robbery takes property from owners; charity gives it to nonowners. How is cruelty to the vulnerable – to the stranger, the homeless one – a form of robbery?

Property and Righteousness
Al tonu ish et akhiv. Do not, any of you, oppress your brother or your sister (Lev. [*Vayikra*] 25:14). This commandment in the twenty-fifth chapter of Leviticus is the source of much of the Jewish law dealing with the marketplace. The Talmud (the repository of Jewish law derived from the Torah) allows for market relationships but tempers self-interest with mutual obligation and support. It requires us to see others as our brothers and sisters. It requires us to see them as created in the image of God. This has consequences for the Jewish view of property.

TZEDAKAH
Although the Torah (the five books of Moses) recognizes the institution of private property, it also contains numerous admonitions to share property with those who have none. Over and over again, we are commanded to look out for the widow, the orphan, the stranger, and the poor. What distinguishes these individuals from others is their lack of access to property. Yet, in the face of this need, those who do have such access have an ongoing obligation to "open your hand to the poor." This obligation extends to everyone in the community who is without property. It also included the tribe of Levi, the priests who, unlike the other tribes, were not given land. "And the Levite, because he has no part nor inheritance with you, and the stranger, and the orphan, and the widow, who are inside your gates, shall come, and shall

eat and be satisfied; that the Lord your God may bless you in all the work of your hand which you do." The widow, the orphan, and the stranger are mentioned together at least a dozen times in the *Tanakh* (the Jewish Bible). The word *stranger* alone appears at least one hundred times, as we are repeatedly commanded to care for the stranger (the sojourner, the homeless one). "The stranger who resides with you shall be as one of your citizens; you shall love him as yourself, for you were strangers in the land of Egypt: I am the Lord your God."[28]

The obligation to care for those in need is not a matter of charity. It is not a matter of generosity alone or pity or selflessness. It is a matter of justice. The word in Hebrew that came to mean "charity" is *tzedakah* (צדקה), which means righteousness or justice. *Tzedek* (צדק) is justice and a *tzaddik* (צדיק) is a righteous person. The duty to provide support for those in need is a matter of justice, not a matter of choice. The obligation to share one's income with the poor is not a matter of grace or choice; it is an obligation. We are commanded to act with justice, giving the poor the portion that belongs to them. The wealth provided by God is meant not only for "the needs and wants of the private owner, [but] is also meant to be used to satisfy the needs of the poor. . . . So society acquires a property right in the wealth of the individual to provide, through compulsory acts of taxation, the social and charitable needs of its members." *Tzedakah* is therefore not merely an exhortation to be generous. "Nonparticipation in such funding [of the needs of the poor] becomes tantamount to theft, either from the recipients of the funding or from the other participants who now have to provide a greater share."[29]

Why does this obligation exist? The passage quoted earlier gives two reasons: "you were strangers in the land of Egypt" and "I am the Lord your God." You were strangers in the land of Egypt; indeed, you were slaves. You know what it is like to be dispossessed. You know the heart of the stranger. "You shall not oppress a stranger, for you know the feelings of the stranger, having yourselves been strangers in the land of Egypt."[30] "I am the Lord your God" who led you out of Egypt. But for the grace of God, you would be there still. You must see yourself in the stranger's eyes. God brought you out of Egypt to come to the desert and receive the Torah at Mount Sinai, to create a covenant with God, to undertake the obligation to live a collective and individual life of goodness, and to undertake the work of continuing Creation by repairing the world (tikkun olam; תיקון עולם). The obligation to take care of the stranger is just that: an obligation, based on a commandment from God. It is not a matter of individual grace, but rather a part of the structure of the world. It is a foundation of sustainable, honorable human relationships, acceptable to God, which recognize that each individual was created in the image of God. Jews are commanded to act as if each of us was standing at Sinai, receiving the Torah. This gift imposes obligations, personal responsibilities "to do justice, love mercy, and walk humbly with your God" (Mic. 6:8).

The Mishnah identifies the mediocre person as one who strictly protects property rights, one who says "What is mine is mine and what is yours is yours." Such a person is not prepared to assist others or "recognize a social obligation in view of the wealth in his possession." The Mishnah goes on to note that "Some say this is the mark of the people of Sodom."[31] Ezekiel tells us: "Only this was the sin of your sister Sodom: arrogance! She and her daughters had plenty of bread and untroubled tranquillity; yet she did not support the poor and the needy. In their haughtiness, they committed abomination before Me; and so I removed them, as you saw."[32] "The Sodomite view of absolute private property rejects any obligations to assist others, which is contrary to the Jewish concept of limited private-property rights."[33]

The obligation to provide for those in need does not remove from the needy the obligation to take care of themselves. Indeed, the obligation to give tzedakah is so essential to the structure of just social relations that even the poor are required to give tzedakah, in order to acknowledge the needs of others.[34] It is crucial to self-respect, to a sense of humanity, to see oneself as needed by others and as capable of responding and helping.

Mutual care does not abolish the obligation to look out for oneself and to engage in the work of repairing the world. Indeed, the greatest form of charity (tzedakah) is to enable the recipient to become self-sufficient.[35] As Maimonides recognized, "The highest degree of charity . . . is to strengthen the hand of another so that the poor one is able to be independent and no longer needy."[36]

GLEANINGS

"The earth is the Lord's and all that it holds, the world and its inhabitants" (Ps. 24:1). The land and its fruits are divine gifts, and the fruits of the land cannot be withheld from those who need them. The story of Joseph recounts his foresight in storing grain for the years of famine so that everyone could make it through the rough times. So too are individual owners commanded to set aside a portion for the poor. Property owners are commanded not to reap to the edges of the field (*pe'ah*),[37] not to pick up grain or grapes that have been dropped in the course of harvesting (gleanings or *leket*),[38] and not to return to the field to retrieve "forgotten sheaves (*shikhechah*)."[39] Those property elements are owned by the widow, the orphan, the stranger, and the poor — those who have no access to land of their own or whose family ties have been shattered. They are not a matter of charity and they do not constitute a transfer from the landowner to the dispossessed. Rather, they are the share of God's bounty belonging to the landless.[40]

My favorite is the commandment concerning *shikhechah*, forgotten sheaves. There they are — harvested, tied up, standing in the field — and one walks off the field, *without them?* There is an implication that one *should* forget some. Similarly with *pe'ah:* the landowner cannot refuse to plant the area along the edges of the field. The owner *must* plant because the poor have a right to their share of the harvest. They are part owners of the land and its produce, and the labor of the owner is partly for their benefit. Owners are dependent on nonowners respecting their claims on land. For this reason, the owner is not entitled to monopolize the land in a way that keeps its produce from being available to sustain all human beings in the community. Because each is created in the image of God, each is entitled to a share in God's bounty.

In the Book of Ruth, Naomi and her husband, Elimelech, and two sons, Mahlon and Chilion, travel away from Israel to a foreign land in which the sons marry. Tragedy strikes and the husband and two sons die. Naomi, the widow, tells her daughters-in-law that they are free to return home to their families while she will return to the land of Israel. One daughter agrees to go home, but Ruth insists on going back to Israel with Naomi. Naomi and Ruth thus return to Naomi's homeland as landless widows. Naomi sends Ruth out to the fields to gather the gleanings so that they may have food.

The rabbis tell us that there was a reason that all the men in the family died. Naomi's husband, Elimelech, was a wealthy man but left Israel with his family during time of famine in the hope of a better life elsewhere. When they went, they took their wealth with them. Naomi's husband, and perhaps Naomi herself, withheld sustenance from others, causing great suffering. His death and the death of his sons is recounted to emphasize the importance of the obligation to care for others in times of need. The result of his selfishness was that his wife and his daughter-in-law became dependent on the gleanings in the field that he would not give to others.[41]

As with the stories of the Flood and the destruction of Sodom, the Torah emotionally portrays the importance of the obligations of owners to non-owners. There but for the grace of God . . .

JUBILEE

Obligations to give *tzedakah* and to leave food for the poor in the fields are supplemented by the duty to leave the land fallow every seven years – a period corresponding to the seven days of the week, ending with Shabbat, the Sabbath. The seventh year is a "sabbatical" year (*Shmitah*) for the land. In that year, the produce of the land is common property. "Now the Sabbath-yield of the land (is) for you, for eating, for you, for your servant and for your handmaid, for your hired-hand and for your resident-settler who sojourn with you" (Lev. [*Vayikra*] 25:6). The produce of the land in that year is not privately owned; whatever grows in the field is owned by everyone.

The Sabbath ensured that everyone had a day of rest: it democratized leisure. The *Shmitah* year makes each one acknowledge that the true owner of the land is God. The Sabbath rest marks a holy time when the poorest of the poor are entitled to feel like kings and queens. And in the Sabbath year, what grows is owned by all, the better to remind us that no one is more important than another in the eyes of God.

The fiftieth year following "seven Sabbath-cycles of years" is the Sabbatical or Jubilee (*Yovel*) Year. The Jubilee Year is marked by the freeing of slaves, the renouncing of debts, and the redistribution of land. In that year, "You shall proclaim release [liberty] throughout your land for all its inhabitants. It shall be a jubilee for you: each of you shall return to your holding and each of you shall return to your family" (Lev. [*Vayikra*] 25:10).

In the Book of Numbers (*Bamidbar*), the tribes of Israel are duly counted. Why? One answer is that everyone counts. Each one was created in the image of God and each one has the responsibilities and rights that attend that status. The counting was done also to determine how much land to give each tribe; the larger tribes received more land. Every fifty years, those who lost their property to debt could return home to their land and to their families. Their land was restored to them. Attention to the right of each one extends to understanding the interaction, the mutual dependence, of each person on each other.

According to the Torah, the land is not "owned" by individuals. It is instead owned by God and given in trust. Use of the land puts one in continual relation to God. The land cannot be used in a way that is detrimental to God's law. The law presented in the Torah thus suggests a variety of strategies for ensuring that each one in the community has access to property.

It is not clear that the Jubilee system was ever followed. But it remains a moral framework whose principles are designed to affect economic relations. This system protects the rights of owners. But it also ensures that the inequalities associated with ownership are mitigated by multiple strategies to allow others access and that inequalities that emerge over time are counteracted by periodic redistribution intended to ensure that each one has a home and a means of livelihood.

LIVELIHOOD AS A LIMIT
ON ECONOMIC COMPETITION

The Talmud – the compilation of Jewish law based on interpretation of the Torah – developed an entire legal system relating to civil affairs, including family and business relations. The Talmud says that "It is permitted to set up shop alongside shop, grain mill alongside grain mill, bath house alongside bath house, and the existing firms cannot prevent it. The new entrepreneurs can argue that you conduct your business on your property, and I do the same." [42] But the right to engage in economic competition ends if it has the effect of putting the first firm out of business entirely. Rashi goes so far as to consider a substantial loss of income by the first firm as unwarranted and impermissible. This principle is the implementation of "You shall love your neighbor." [43]

Protection of each one's ability to earn a living, or to be supported by others through *tzedakah,* limits the kinds of conduct that are allowable in market relations. Employers have an ironclad duty to pay their employees' wages on time, "for he is poor and unto it [the wages] he turns his soul" (Deut. [*D'varim*] 24:15). Maimonides emphasized that a righteous person "has to be in truth and in faith."

> His yes is to be yes and his no, no; he forces himself to be exact in calculations when he is paying but is willing to be lenient when others are his debtors. . . . He should keep his obligations in commerce even where the law allows him to withdraw or retract, so that his word is his bond; but if others have obligations to him, he should deal mercifully, forgiving and extending credit. One should be careful not to deprive one's neighbor of his livelihood, even where this is legal and efficient, so that one does not cause hardship and anguish. He who does all these things is the one referred to by the prophet Isaiah when he said in God's name, "You, Israel, are My servant, in whom I take pride" (Isa. 49:3). [44]

Obligations to others with whom one forms a market relationship are acknowledged to prevent "oppression." The Torah forbids taking a millstone as security for a loan, for example (Deut. [*D'varim*] 24:6) because it is needed to grind grain for flour. Basic necessities, such as a pillow or a cloak, taken as security for a loan must be returned each night (Exod. [*Shemot*] 22:25–26).

Property and Dignity

> *And if you sell something to your neighbor, or buy something from your neighbor's hand, do not oppress one another.*
> — Lev. (*Vayikra*) 25:14

Al tonu ish et-akhiv (אל־תונו איש את־אחיו). Do not wrong your brother. The rabbis of the Talmud have interpreted the prohibition of oppression (*ona'ah*; אונאה) to apply to both financial oppression and verbal oppression. The rules of fraud prohibit both overcharging and taking unfair advantage in market transactions.[45] Such practices constitute a form of theft. And oppression does not only apply to price fraud (*ona'ah mamon*) but to fraud committed by words (*ona'ah d'varim*). This second kind of oppression prohibits the consumer from using a store only for the purpose of discovering prices; wasting an owner's time when one does not intend to do business robs the owner of his or her time. This is considered a form of business dishonesty. Beyond this, it is considered a form of oppression to criticize a convert or a repentant sinner.[46] And this form of oppression – oppression by words, by gossip, by false dealing – is considered worse than the other kind.[47]

What the Talmud teaches us is that the rules about buying and selling are rules about human dignity. The fact that one concept – *ona'ah* – encompasses both fraudulent dealing and verbal abuse suggests that these wrongs have a common structure. They are wrongs to the person. Failing to respect the property of another wrongs that person because it fails to treat the other person as one created in the image of God. Gossiping about another person, hurting another's reputation or feelings, also robs that person of their dignity. The rules of property in Jewish law are encompassed in the Golden Rule: Treat others as you would wish to be treated. Respect the property of others; respect the right of others to acquire property. The central concept of *ona'ah* demands that each person be allowed to participate fully in social life by establishing some type of ownership, and that dealings of one with another be such that one can be proud of how one has acted.

Aaron Feuerstein was not selfless. His decision to protect his employees' jobs when his factory burned down and to attempt to sustain them financially in the interim was partly a decision to maintain a profitable business, with all the benefits that accrued to him and his family. He used his property to make money for himself and his family, and he was and remains a shrewd businessman. "Other CEOs feel I'm sort of a stupid guy who doesn't know what to do with his excess money," Feuerstein acknowledged. He continued:

> But treating the workers fairly is good for the shareholder. I consider our workers an asset, not a cuttable expense. The quality of Polartec [the synthetic fabric manufactured by Feuerstein's mill] is what I'm selling. By treating the people the way I'd want them to treat me, they make that quality. When you do the right thing, you'll probably end up more profitable than if you did wrong.[48]

Feuerstein did not feel free to act without concern for the interests of his workers and the community in which he lived. Part of his motivation was to protect his own economic interests, but part of it was also to act fairly to the people with whom he had structured long-term relationships and who were dependent on him for their livelihood. He recognized that he was dependent on them, too. He recognized the part they played in his own economic success and he figured out a way he could make money and still comply with his commitments. This might, in the long run, serve him well economically. Yet Feuerstein considered himself to have an obligation to act in this way even if it cost him some money – although not if it would substantially harm him. The work and the good will of the workers had made him rich. He could not, in good conscience, abandon them, when an economically feasible alternative seemed to exist. He used his property in a manner that was compatible with the ability of others to become property owners. He treated his workers as if they had a form of tenure – of ownership – in their jobs. He treated them, in a sense, like the partners they were.

The law did not require Feuerstein to act as he did. He acted pursuant to a Talmudic maxim that one should act *lifnim mishurat hadin*, beyond the letter of the law. Some of the rabbis of the Talmud believed that the Flood was caused by individuals overlooking "forbidden yet legal acts."[49] Acting within the letter of law can wreak havoc. As the Talmud recounts, "Since one is not liable for the theft of less than a *shaveh prutah* [the smallest denomination of money possible, similar to a penny], each man, woman, and child in the town picked one olive out of the silo of a farmer till none were left."[50] For this reason, although such acts are not, technically speaking, illegal, they are nonetheless prohibited to the law-abiding person.

In addition, rabbinical courts have often turned such equitable principles into enforceable legal rules.[51] Because of the translation of these ethical obligations into enforceable legal duties, Jewish law grew to prohibit treatment of workers as "simply factors of production."[52] For example, modern rabbinical courts in Israel have required employers of long-time employees to make severance payments when they are laid off due to the employer's economic circumstances.[53]

The importance of acting "beyond the letter of the law" is illustrated by a remarkable Talmudic passage known as *mishe parah*. It occurs in the midst of a tractate developing rules about property and exchange. The rabbis state the general rule that, when one buys goods, it is the transfer of the goods, and not the transfer of the money, that clinches the deal and makes it irrevocable. If I agree to sell you my car and give you possession of my car, you own the car and are obligated to give me the purchase price, but if you give me the money first, either one of us can back out of the deal. The rule is that the transfer of the car is the act that establishes the obligation. This means that a promise, without transfer of the good, is not legally enforceable. In traditional Talmudic law, there is no obligation to make good on a promise unless other actions happen, such as the transfer of the goods.

But the rabbis were not happy with this rule. It would mean, for example, that I could back out of the deal even if you have already paid me the money for the car and even if I promised to sell it to you, and you were relying on getting it that day. The Talmud reports the debates among the rabbis, and tells us: "But they said: the One who punished the people of the generation of the flood and the generation of the dispersion [at the Tower of Babel] will punish the one who does not stand by his word." [54] Even though it was not traditionally seen as illegal (meaning not encompassed within a rule established in the Torah or the Talmud) the rabbis felt so strongly about the importance of keeping one's word – even when one was not legally required to do so – that they pronounced a curse on anyone who did not.

In effect, the rabbis said that the practice of promise breaking was a sin so terrible, so offensive to the dignity of the person and to the right ordering of human relationships, that it represented the kind of evil that led God to bring the Flood and to scatter the peoples of the earth. The law-abiding person does not only do what is legally required but what the principles underlying the law and ethical conduct require. Some of these principles are so fundamentally important that they circle back and become part of the law. Thus the rabbinic courts imposed obligations on employers who lay off workers that go beyond the contractual obligations. This process is a familiar one in English and U.S. legal history and is part of the way that equitable principles developed by the chancery courts became enforceable rules of law despite their previous nonenforcement by the common law courts.

Christianity

The obligations imposed in Judaism on both property owners and the community as a whole are not particular to that religion. The Christian tradition focuses less on the concept of obligation and more on the concept of empathy for those in need. The result is quite similar. Christianity teaches that it is incumbent on human beings to pay special attention to the poor and the downtrodden. "The poor are robbed of justice," writes Milner Ball, in an essay on a text in the Book of

Mark.[55] According to the Christian tradition, attending to those in need has consequences for how we should live our lives and how we should build our social world.

The National Conference of Catholic Bishops began their *Pastoral Letter on Catholic Social Teaching and the U.S. Economy*, entitled *Economic Justice for All*, by quoting the parable of the Last Judgment. "For I was hungry and you gave me food, I was thirsty and you gave me drink. . . . As often as you did it for one of my least brothers, you did it for me" (Matt. 25:35–40).[56] The *Letter* notes that the first public utterance of Jesus was "The Spirit of the Lord is upon me, therefore he has anointed me. He has sent me to bring glad tidings to the poor" (Luke 4:18). "Jesus takes the side of those most in need," the bishops tell us. "In the Last Judgment, so dramatically described in St. Matthew's Gospel, we are told that we will be judged according to how we respond to the hungry, the thirsty, the naked, the stranger."[57]

The obligation to care for the needy is part of a larger obligation. "*Every economic decision and institution must be judged in light of whether it protects or undermines the dignity of the human person.*" This principle mandates that each person, sacred in the eyes of God, is entitled to participate in economic life. "Basic justice demands that people be assured a minimum level of participation in the economy. It is wrong for a person or group to be excluded unfairly or to be unable to participate or contribute to the economy." This means, for example, that "people who are both able and willing, but cannot get a job, are deprived of the participation that is so vital to human development."[58]

The insight underlying this vision is similar to the basis of obligation for Jews and Moslems. "When we deal with each other, we should do so with the sense of awe that arises in the presence of something holy and sacred. For that is what human beings are: we are created in the image of God" (Gen. 1:27).[59] This focus on the sacredness of the person connects love for God with love of human beings. "When asked what was the greatest commandment, Jesus quoted the age-old Jewish affirmation of faith that God alone is One and to be loved with the whole heart, mind, and soul (Deut. 6:4–5) and immediately adds: 'You shall love your neighbor as yourself' (Lev. 19:18; Mark 12:28–34)."[60] Love of God and love of one's neighbor are not separate; they implicate each other and one cannot exist without the other.

The injunction to care for each other means both that each person is entitled to a "share of earthly goods sufficient for oneself and one's family," as the Second Vatican Council stated, and that each person is obligated to be an "*active and productive participant in the life of society and that society has a duty to enable them to participate in this way.*"[61] Ensuring basic requirements of justice not only obligates individuals to give charity; it obligates the community to shape the institutions that govern economic life, establishing relationships that distribute power and wealth equitably.[62] A just economic system calls for the creation of jobs that pay adequate wages and would establish *for each person* the "possibility of property ownership."[63]

STEWARDSHIP

These teachings are not confined to Catholicism. Christian teaching has long included attention to the needs of the poor or oppressed. As Anthony Cook explains, a goal of Christian religious life is to "make love real in the world."[64] Quoting Walter Rauschenbusch, Cook notes that this requires that we "give up 'the opportunity to exploit men,' draining them for our own ease and convenience." Martin Luther King's conception of the Beloved Community rested on the "willingness to see the other as an extension of oneself." For this reason, as Cook notes, King rejected the idea that "human rights" should be subordinate to "the rights of property." "A life is sacred," wrote King. "Property is intended to serve life, and no matter how much we surround it with rights and respect, it has no personal being. It is part of the earth man walks on; it is not man."[66]

William Stringfellow, a Christian lawyer who worked with the poor, explained that "the Christian is to be found in his work and witness in the world among those for whom no one else cares – the poor, the sick, the imprisoned, the misfits, the homeless, the orphans and beggars." There is a reason for the identification of the Christian with those who have nothing or who are vulnerable. "The presence of the Christian among the outcasts is the way in which the Christian represents, concretely, the ubiquity and universality of the intercession of Christ for all men."[67]

Peter J. Gomes explains the Christian concept of stewardship. Stewardship "implies that one's money is not really one's own; one holds it in trust from God and for the benefit of others."[68] Wealth is a "gift from God" and is "only loaned to the one who takes its benefit on earth." Wealth is a "means rather than an end."[69] Gomes explains that those who confuse wealth with success or happiness miss the point of real success and real happiness. He quotes Matthew 6:19–21: "Do not lay up for yourselves treasures on earth, where moth and rust consume and where thieves break in and steal, but lay up yourselves treasures in heaven, where neither moth nor rust consumes and where thieves do not break in and steal. For where your treasure is, there will your heart be also."

The Christian view is that riches are granted as a gift from God to enable individuals to live a good life that includes attention to the needs of others. "Wealth is not what you have; wealth is what you have been given that enables you to give to others."[70] Those who have are obligated to those who have not. "Upon those who have wealth there is a burden of responsibility to use it wisely and not only for themselves." The wealthy must be "generous in proportion to their wealth" because "to whom much is given much is expected."[71]

Jim Wallis echoes these messages. "[T]he biblical prophets encourage us to be suspicious of concentrations of wealth and power [and] especially to be sensitive to the poor, the disenfranchised, the stranger, and the outsider. The Bible radically relativizes all claims to ownership and domination of land and resources by asserting that 'the Earth is the Lord's' and its abundance intended to be shared by all of God's children."[72] It does so because each person is precious in the eyes of God and "just as you did not do it to one of the least of these, you did not do it to me."[73] Wallis notes: "Jesus is here asking, 'How much do you love me? I'll know how much you love me by how you love those who are the most vulnerable.' "[74] The love of others is connected with, entailed by, the love of God. "John's letters [explain] that if we do not love our neighbor in need, we simply do not love God."[75]

Islam
The Islamic tradition builds on both Christianity and Judaism. Like the Jewish tradition, the Moslem approach to charity includes both voluntary and compulsory components.

ZAKAT
Zakat is a form of charity that is mandated and of a calculated amount. Once one has satisfied regular needs and expenses, one is obligated to give a minimum of 2.5 percent of one's surplus wealth and earnings at the end of the year.[76] The obligation is based on the notion that individuals are part of the community.[77] As the prophet Muhammad said, "like the organs of the body, if one suffers then all others rally in response." *Zakat* "represents the unbreakable bond between members of the community."[78]

Zakat is understood as the entitlement of the poor to the wealth of those who have enough to share. As with Judaism, the tradition respects private property but does not allow owners to hoard their wealth in ways that leave others destitute. The word *zakat* means "purification," "growth," or "sweetening" and links giving with the actions necessary to live in a holy manner.[79]

All wealth is believed to belong to God and is held by human beings in trust. As in Judaism, individuals are entitled to own property, but they are not entitled to consider their interests alone.[80] The relationship between human beings and God and the "social responsibility of a Muslim, require that property be used not only for one's personal advantage and benefit, but also for the advantage and benefit of the community." The right of ownership is qualified by the "rights of the needy." "The Prophet was heard to say: 'He cannot be a believer. He

cannot be a believer. He cannot be a believer.' When asked 'Who?',
the Prophet answered: 'He who sleeps the night with a full stomach,
while his neighbour is hungry.' "[81]

SADAQAH

Over and above *zakat* is *sadaqah,* or voluntary giving. Although *sadaqah* is nominally voluntary, there is a moral obligation to give.[82] The
prophet Muhammad said, "Charity is a necessary obligation for every
Muslim."[83] This obligation extends to every Muslim, even the need-
iest.

> When asked, "What if a person has nothing?" the Prophet replied: "He
> should work with his own hands for his benefit and then give something out
> of such earnings in charity." The Companions then asked: "What if he is not
> able to work?" The Prophet said: "He should help poor and needy persons."
> The Companions further asked: "What if he cannot do even that?" The
> Prophet said: "He should urge others to do good."[84]

The Qur'an lists eight categories of persons who are eligible to receive
sadaqah: "the poor, the destitute, those employed to collect the funds,
those whose hearts are to be reconciled, captives to obtain their freedom, debtors, those engaged in holy war, and wayfarers."[85] Those
who are vulnerable are entitled to support. This includes those who
are needy in both body and spirit.

Proclaim Liberty Throughout the Land

According to Avivah Gottlieb Zornberg, Jacob is the first person in
the Torah specifically described both as a worker (*oved*) and as one
who loves (*ohev*) his spouse. Work is necessary to continue the creation of the world and it is connected with love. The Biblical idiom
for property ownership is *va-yehi lo,* literally "there was to him" (Gen.
[*Bereishit*] 30:43). Property is connected to the person and the one
who has nothing is less than free. "The poor man is like a dead man,"
say the rabbis.[86] Someone who is "needy of others" for basic suste-

nance cannot function as a full member of the community. Specifically, and devastatingly, he will find it difficult to pray. "He will be excruciatingly aware of the gaze of others, which will induce a fatal self-consciousness in him. His prayers will then become affected."[87] The one who is dispossessed is, for that reason, not free. This is why the *Yovel*, the Jubilee Year that comes every fifty years, connects the liberation of bondsmen (slaves, indentured workers) with the return of everyone to their homes, their land, and their families. To return to one's family, one must have a home to go back to, and to have a home to return to, one must have property where a home can be.

"Proclaim liberty throughout the land," declares the text of Leviticus, connecting liberty with the practice of ensuring that each one in the community is an owner of property or is a member of family that owns property.[88] In this vision, dispossession is connected with slavery. Feuerstein treated his workers like people; he valued them. "I consider the employees standing in front of me here the most valuable asset that Malden Mills has. I don't consider them, like some companies do, as an expense that can be cut."[89] To be dispossessed is to know what it is like to be devalued, cut out, excluded from the world of mutual regard. To be an owner is to receive a gift; to be an owner who is also a *mensch* is to know that the gift is not for you alone.

CHAPTER FOUR

Rent

*To choose to circumscribe oneself, to take responsibility for
one's web of dependences, is both enriching and demanding. It
is a surrender of immunity. But the immunity is a superficial
kind, fantastic and, in the end, untenable. It rests on a refusal
to take reliance as a source of obligation.*[1]

— Jedediah Purdy, *For Common Things*

*What was it about that night
connection — in an isolating age.*[2]

— Jonathan Larson, *Rent*

The back cover of the videotape edition of the movie *The Full Monty*
describes it as a "hilarious, heartfelt comedy." "Six unemployed men,"
the jacket relates, "inspired by a touring group of male strippers, de-
cide they can make a small fortune" by going "the full monty" and
stripping "completely naked." The theme is one of personal triumph
as "these six friends discover the inner strength to bare it all in front
of the world."[3] It is a description that promises laughter, a hint of titil-
lation, and no small amount of emotional satisfaction. Critical excla-
mation marks abound. "Irresistible . . . hilarious!" gushes Janet Maslin
of the *New York Times.* "Heart-warming fun!" opines Kevin Thomas
of the *Los Angeles Times* in cheerful, red letters. "Roaringly funny!"
blares Peter Travers of *Rolling Stone* magazine.

The only hint that anything is amiss among these cheery descrip-
tions is that the men, all of them, are "unemployed." This is why these
men are willing to strip naked in front of their friends and neighbors.
They have lost their jobs at the steel mill and they are desperate. The
first time Gaz and Dave meet Lomper (the security guard at the

broken-down factory) he is abandoning his elderly mother and is trying to kill himself in his car with carbon monoxide fumes. Gerald, their old foreman, has been pretending to go to work for six months because he cannot bear to tell his wife that he has lost his job. Gaz is terrified because his ex-wife has threatened to go to court to take away his right to see his son unless he can find a way to make his child support payments.

I do not mean to be a wet blanket. *The Full Monty is* funny; it *is* heartwarming. But it is not *just* heartwarming; it is also heart*breaking*. The marketing of this movie reflects a peculiar disinclination – or more likely an unwillingness – to face the not-so-funny fact that these men are willing to do this thing, not because they are on personal quests for fulfillment, but because they are at the end of their respective ropes. They have nothing left to lose.

The movie works, of course, because their situation is a familiar one. We have seen it happen. We can understand what they are going through. We can imagine what it would be like to lose your job and not be able to find another. The dramatic tension in the movie comes from the feeling these men have that they have no alternative. After much hesitation, they go through with it. They do this and they make a small bundle. But this was a one-shot deal. And the question is: What happens when they've used up what they made? What then?

"I've Lost Everything"

What then? It is hard to face this: this dark underside of our prosperous, flexible, global economy, the benefits of which are unevenly spread. *The Full Monty* is a subtle critique of the circumstances that gave rise to the willingness of these men to do what would otherwise be unthinkable for them. It is also a celebration of solidarity as a response to these circumstances. These men all hit rock bottom in different ways, lying to themselves and others, before taking the risk to offer *themselves,* entrepreneurially, and revealingly, and to gain self-respect in the process of risking communal scrutiny. The story centers around the human consequences of unemployment and the need for mutual support when times are rough. Audiences understood all this;

they got the deeper meaning. As critic Roger Ebert wrote, underneath it all, *The Full Monty* is about the "fight for dignity . . . and self-respect."[4] *The Full Monty* was a surprise hit and a big moneymaker — in fact, it was the "most successful British film ever."[5] People learned about it through word of mouth, not through massive Hollywood-style promotion.

The characters in *The Full Monty* are resilient and we applaud them for this. But resilience is a plausible response to dislocation only when there is a realistic alternative to despair. *Brassed Off* is a darker version of the *Full Monty* story. This time it's a coal pit in England and this time despair is a bigger part of the dramatic picture. The company has given the workers a choice that is not much of a choice. They can give up their jobs and accept "redundancy" in return for a one-time cash payment, or they can take their chances with a review process almost certain to end with closure anyway and wind up with half as much money. The consequences of the closing will be catastrophic. No new jobs are on the horizon. The miners fight among themselves. They resist but they cannot find a way out. Again, we have marriages breaking up, tension between husbands and wives, another attempted suicide. "Look at me," Phil sobs, after trying to hang himself from the steel girders of the processing plant. "I've lost everything . . . wife, kids, house, job, self-respect, hope."[6] The miners and their families are in a tunnel with no light at the end. As far as they can tell, the tunnel does not go anywhere; the path they are on is a dead end.

The English word for layoffs is eerie: *redundancy*. The *New Shorter Oxford Dictionary* defines *redundancy* as the "condition of being surplus to an organization's staffing requirements; loss of a job as a result of reorganization, mechanization, etc."[7] "A few years and men won't exist except in zoos," says Dave in *The Full Monty*. "I mean, we're not needed no more, are we? Obsolete, dinosaurs, yesterday's news. . . . We're scrap."[8] Again and again, workers are being told that they do not matter.

The workers in *Brassed Off* vote to agree to "accept redundancy" and closure of the coal mine because most of them think this is the best deal they can get. The main characters play in a brass band that has existed for more than a hundred years and that participates in local competitions. Their conductor, Danny, thinks they can win the annual event and exhorts them to do their best. How they can afford to keep playing is a central issue. They do so, in the face of despair at the imminent closing, and do well enough to enter the finals at the Albert Hall in London. Music gives them dignity and meaning that is being robbed from them. But they don't have enough money even to make the trip to London until a management employee who had been trying to get the company to keep the pit open quits her job and gives them the money. "I don't want it," she says. "It's tainted money." They take it and go to the finals. They play their hearts out and win the competition. Danny steps up to give a speech and refuses the award in order to get attention to the plight of his town. He rails against a governmental and economic system that treats the miners as disposable. These men, he says, are "just ordinary common garden honest decent human beings and not one of them with an ounce of bloody hope left."[9]

Policy makers should recognize the human costs of property systems that are so focused on profit maximization that they ignore the costs they impose on individuals, families, and communities. This does not mean that factories can never close and workers can never be fired. It does mean that the system, as a whole, must ensure that jobs are available where people live or that there is some alternative way to obtain work. "I used to like to go to work but they shut it down," sings Mark Knopfler of Dire Straits. "I've got a right to go to work but there's no work here to be found."[10]

When New England's two largest banks announced in March 1999 that they would merge to create the nation's eighth-largest bank (in a deal worth $16 billion – yes, *billion*), they also announced that they would eliminate five thousand jobs.[11] Reactions to the announcement were mixed. "By increasing in size, banks achieve the economies of scale that allow us to invest more in technology and people," said a Fleet spokesperson.[12] Those economies are partly, but not entirely, achieved by the elimination of jobs and of "duplicative" branch offices. Will there really be an increase in investment or just a decrease in competition and an increase in profits? Will this new megabank invest in local communities in amounts that will offset the proposed job losses? How do we measure the social effects of such downsizings and mergers? Perhaps those laid off will find new jobs; the job market was tight in the summer of 1999. But it is not clear that everyone laid off will find a comparable job at comparable wages close to home. Is the deal being financed partly by sacrificing those workers? Who benefits and who is harmed by downsizing?[9]

Danny's final speech in *Brassed Off* complains not only about the destruction of an "entire industry" but the destruction of "our communities, our homes, our lives, all in the name of progress and for a few lousy bob."[13] "Free enterprise" has many social benefits. But a system that is indifferent to job stability and availability causes social dislocation. Such dislocation disrupts the very communities that are the source of the stability needed to imbue individuals with a work ethic and basic social values. And a system that has no safety net for those who are most vulnerable to economic change may be a prosperous one, but it is not an admirable one. We do not cheer for such a system when we face the consequences of profit at the expense of humanity.

Profits and Prophets

Popular culture in the United States is replete with criticism of a corporate culture that puts profits ahead of any other considerations. The film *The Rainmaker* recounts the fight of a young, inexperienced lawyer trying to get insurance benefits from an indifferent insurance company which refuses to pay for a procedure that would likely have saved a young man's life. The company refuses to pay for the procedure and the young man dies. There is no question of sympathy for the insurance company. We learn that it is taking money from its customers with no intent to pay when it is contractually obligated to do so. The trial reveals that the company's policy was to deny benefits every time a claim was made on the hope that the claimant would just go away. The president of the company seems to have no sense that real people are depending on him to get the medical care they need. He is corrupt; he is unwilling even to give customers the benefits for which they have paid. Profits for him over everything. *Over everything.* He is even willing to ignore the property rights and the very lives of others.

Matt Damon's quiet performance in *The Rainmaker* plays down the sense of outrage the situation might engender. Instead, he emphasizes the young lawyer's incredulity that the company would act this way. He learns what happened but he simply cannot believe it. It is a story about his loss of innocence. But it is also a story about the potential of law to respond to injustice, to protect the little guy against the big corporation.

In the truly funny film *Big Business,* Lilly Tomlin and Bette Midler play two sets of twins mixed up at birth. A rich couple is driving in a rural Appalachian town when the wife goes into labor. They stop at a company hospital which refuses to help her because she is not an employee of the company. The husband walks across the street and buys the company (and, as it happens, the entire town), and returns as the new boss so his wife can give birth. A poor local couple enters the hospital at the same time. Two sets of twins are born. The twins are mixed up and there is one Lilly (Rose) and one Bette (Sadie) in each family. Years later the rich Sadie is planning to sell the company and the rest of the town to an Italian magnate who intends to close the factory and strip-mine the town. The poor Sadie and Rose go to the city to stop this. After some hilarious twin mix-ups, rich Rose and poor Sadie stand up at the stockholders' meeting to convince them to vote against the sale.

The audience is clearly expected to root for the small town. Rose and Sadie appeal to the stockholders' humanity. Do they really want to be a party to the strip mining of a beautiful, rural town, to destroy a way of life that is valuable, that the stockholders themselves value? When this line of argument seems not to be working, Sadie suggests they think about the terrible publicity the company will face when the public finds out what they did. Vote against the sale, she says, "to save your own asses!"[14] Again, the movie sets up a contest between the idea of making money at all costs and the value of preserving the small town way of life – the value, in other words, of other values.

Even the full-length children's animated feature of *The Jetsons* sets up a conflict between a company (Spacely Sprockets) and some cute space creatures who live underground on an asteroid. The company is mining the asteroid for material to make "sprockets" and in so doing it is destroying the homes of these cuddly creatures. The creatures resist by sabotaging the machines so that they cannot continue their devastation. George Jetson saves the day by convincing Mr. Spacely to hire the creatures to work the factory and use recycled sprockets rather than mine raw material. In true cartoon fashion, the conflict is not so much resolved as transcended. Cartoon or not, one wonders: Are there ways to obtain the benefits of vigorous economic competition, innovation, and transition while preserving the ability of each person to find a place in this system and live in dignity?

This question is not just a question about property. It is a question about ourselves. In a riveting episode of *Star Trek: The Next Generation,* entitled *The Measure of a Man,* a Starfleet scientist wants to dismantle Data (a conscious, humanoid robot) to find out how he works so they can build more "androids" like him. Data objects because the procedure is likely to erase both his personality and his memories. Starfleet persists: he has no rights, he is a machine, he was constructed, he was made by research funded by Starfleet, he is the property of Starfleet and they can dismantle him if they want to. A trial ensues on the question of whether Data is property or a person. The advocate for the scientist emphasizes the fact that he is a constructed machine, that he can be turned off, that he was not a naturally occurring life form. The defense by Captain Jean-Luc Picard emphasizes Data's consciousness, his resistance, and his humanity.

Midway, it looks as if Starfleet is going to win. And then Guinan (played to great effect by Whoopi Goldberg) asks Captain Picard what Starfleet intends to do if they figure out how to make more "Datas." Well, I guess they will make them, he answers. How many? Guinan wonders. "Mattox could get lucky and create a whole army of Datas, all very valuable," comments Guinan. Data has "proved his value to you. And now he's about to be ruled the property of Starfleet. That should increase his value." If androids are ruled the property of Starfleet and have no rights, they can be controlled by Starfleet and made to do what Starfleet wants, can't they? "Whole generations of dispos-able people," Guinan says. "You're talking about slavery," says Picard. "Oh, I think that's a little harsh," says Guinan. "I don't think that's a little harsh," answers Picard. "I think it's the truth."[15]

Captain Picard returns to the trial and says, We have been asking the wrong question. We cannot answer the question of whether Data is property or a person by asking what he is. We should look to our-selves. What do we want to be? If we treat him as property, what kind of people will we be? What kind of society will we have created? What kind of judgment will history bestow on us? The question, Pi-card says, is not what Data is, but what we are, what we will be, what kind of world we will make. "The decision you reach here today . . . will reveal the kind of a people we are," Picard argues.[16] Data wins the dispute, not because the judge can answer the question of whether he really is or isn't property, but because slavery is an abomination. The question of the scope and range of property rights is answered, finally, by a human choice — a choice between profit at all costs and humanity.

"Connection — in an Isolating Age"

What does it take to connect with others? As Jedediah Purdy asks in his book *For Common Things,* how can we achieve a "sense of being connected rather than alone"?[17] What image of property can recon-cile the world of profit and the world of compassion? In Jonathan Lar-son's rock opera *Rent,* we have a cultural production that asks what the haves owe the have-nots. The story of the opera confronts directly the question of what the relation should be between morality and prop-erty and the place of religion in our relationship to material wealth. I want to analyze the message of *Rent* at some length, looking at both the music and story as they relate to the themes of isolation and connection, property and obligation. Larson's exploration of these themes yields insights surprisingly reminiscent of those suggested by Aaron Feuerstein. We may not expect the values of Orthodox Jews to converge with the values expressed in a commercially successful rock opera. I have been trying to suggest that this convergence is less puz-zling than it appears. We have seen that both American law and American religious traditions embody the idea that owners have obligations as well as rights and that we highly value those who pay attention to the needs of others. And, as we have seen, one of the stock stories in American popular culture is resistance to those who seek profit at any cost, especially human costs. Americans value success but we also judge harshly those who achieve it by sacrificing the humanity of others.

Rent created a sensation when it opened partly because so few Broadway shows have successfully used rock music, and partly because Larson's score is hauntingly beautiful and affecting. Its success is phenomenal. It has been in continuous production on Broadway since 1996 and been presented in numerous other cities and around the world. The intense reaction to the show reflects Larson's attempt to confront the problem of living in a world occupied by the plague of AIDS. The personal agonies of those touched by the disease are underscored in horrific fashion by Larson's own untimely death at the age of thirty-five from an aortic aneurysm on the night of the show's final dress rehearsal.

The intense reaction to *Rent* also reflects Larson's use of characters who are not typical inhabitants of Broadway shows. They are as likely to be gay as straight. They include a recovering heroin addict, a current user, a transvestite, a nightclub stripper, and a "computer-age philosopher." They are also, for the most part, young, with the penchant of the young to ponder questions about the meaning of life that many adults put aside, as though they were resolved. The chorus is composed substantially of homeless people who form the backdrop to everything that happens to the main characters. The story is based on Giacomo Puccini's *La Bohème,* and thus most of the main characters are artists who live in poverty: Mark the filmmaker, Roger the punk rocker, Maureen the performance artist, Angel the street performer, and Collins the "computer-age philosopher." They, unlike most homeless people, have some choice about their poverty. They have chosen to lead a bohemian life on the margins of society. They celebrate this life outside the "mainstream," with the demands and rewards granted artists, and they do so in the face of multiple pressures to "sell out." Larson celebrates them, in all their human complexity. He takes them seriously and he forces us to do so as well.

The reviews of *Rent* have focused on the outsider status of the characters, their struggles with AIDS and drug addiction, and the problems of couples finding love, breaking up, and getting back together, or not. Although some reviews mention the fact that homeless people appear as characters in the play, few have elaborated on the meaning of their role. Nor have reviewers analyzed, or taken seriously, the variety of images and songs in *Rent* that involve both property and law. Yet these images are central to an understanding of the play. Homeless people figure prominently and their comments are interwoven with other stories involving AIDS, drug addiction, and the search for love. Mimi, one of the main characters, eventually winds up living on the street herself. Benny, the landlord, ejects the homeless people squatting on his vacant lot; he also attempts to evict the artists from their loft. The title of the play itself evokes the issue of property, the possibility of eviction, and the threat of homelessness.

Indeed, the plot of the first act revolves around a crucial question: What obligations do we owe the propertyless? The play begins when Benny, the landlord, calls Mark and Roger to demand the last year's rent – rent he knows they cannot pay him. If they do not pay, he will evict them, unless they do one small thing for him. Benny was their roommate until he married into a rich family, bought the building, and became their landlord and the owner of the lot next door. He plans to build a commercial building on the "vacant" property. The only problem is that the lot is occupied by homeless people. Maureen, an ex-roommate of Mark and Roger (and incidentally of Benny himself) is planning to stage a protest against Benny's plan to eject the homeless people from the lot. Benny asks Mark and Roger to convince Maureen to call off her protest. In return for this "one small favor," he offers to drop his eviction threat, let them live in the loft rent free, create a "cyberarts studio" in the building he will construct next door, enable Roger and Mark to share in the rents he will earn when he leases the upper floors of the new building as condos, give Mark and Roger the right to use the studio (free) to do their artistic work, and put it all in writing. "Just stop the protest," Benny says, "and you'll have it made."

Let us be clear about this: Benny is, in effect, offering to make Mark and Roger property owners like himself, with the right to live, rent free, in their home, and the right to collect rents from wealthy tenants, live off those rents, and spend their days doing what they love to do — filmmaking and songwriting. It is an unbelievable offer; it is, to them, as if they had won the lottery. All they need do is this one little thing. It is a small request. They need not help eject the homeless people, they need have no responsibility for that. Benny intends to build the building in any case; their refusal to help will not stop this from happening. It would just be easier for Benny if there were no protest that might garner bad publicity. It is a small thing he asks of them in return for their life's dream. *But they refuse.*

This is a remarkable thing. It is also the plot around which the first act revolves. One would not learn this, however, from reading reviews of the play. Perhaps this is understandable: after all, we live in an age of self-reliance, an age that suggests that poor people have only themselves to blame for their predicament. Nonetheless, I think Larson would not have approved. *Rent* directly confronts the question of whether owners have obligations as well as rights. The title of the play itself, *Rent,* suggests the importance of these issues to Larson.

The play moves from individuals to relationships to social and political life. Larson addresses the problems of individuals (and their friends) facing the horror of AIDS and the challenges involved in "living with" AIDS rather than "dying from" it. He also puts a spotlight on the problem of "selling out" — choosing a career that makes money but demands sacrificing oneself and one's core values, placing oneself and one's economic interests above the obligation to consider the effects of such choices on the most vulnerable among us. Both AIDS and the problem of selling out concern the meaning of life and the possibility of the death of the body or the spirit. Larson responds to the physical and mental plagues by suggesting a way to affirm life. He asks us to live today as if it mattered, as if it were our last day, and he asks us to treat others as if they mattered, as if it were their last day.

He asks us to get beyond ourselves, to see other people, to care about them. In so doing, we will see ourselves. Larson also addresses the dilemmas raised by relationships, among friends, between children and parents, between landlords and tenants, between owners and squatters. He raises the ambiguities of separation and independence as well as the rewards and hazards of love. Larson then asks us to consider the obligations we have to strangers, symbolized by the homeless characters and personified by the Greek chorus. The chorus continually reappears to remind us that during the travails of the artists in their individual lives and relationships, other people exist outside their windows who have no one, nowhere to go, no place to be, no mother to call.

The return of the ideology of self-reliance, the outsider status and stereotyped images of welfare recipients, and the growing impatience with the problems of the homeless, suggest a change in our fundamental conceptions of both property and welfare. *Rent* is about an "America at the end of the millennium" in which allegiance to the new regime of "personal responsibility" is supported by political and academic arguments that government aid for people who find themselves in dire straits only ends up hurting them. There is no need to worry about the poor – even poor children. Tough love is good for them; government action will only makes things worse. Self-reliance or private charity will take up the slack.

Rent is an exploration of and extended comment on these changes in our political culture. What is it that has brought us to the situation in which "you're what you own"? Larson's play profoundly explores the failures of "connection – in an isolating age." At the same time, the central message is that strategies exist to overcome those failures. Connection is possible; "for once I didn't disengage." "Shadows" can give way to "light." Rather than give in to Benny, Roger and Mark join Maureen's protest. In so doing, they remind Benny about what he really values – values that he never gave up but that he had pushed aside. He may tell himself that it's just business; they remind him to listen to his conscience. "You can't quietly wipe out an entire tent city," Roger says, "then watch *It's a Wonderful Life* on TV!" *Rent* makes us confront this disjunction between the values of the market-place and the values associated with the rest of life, including our deepest moral and religious values. How can you watch *It's a Wonderful Life* and then wipe out a tent city? One can believe it will all work out in the long run. But in the short run – now – Christmas bells are ringing, somewhere else, not here. Is that the kind of world we want? Do we want a world where "you're on your own"? If we do, why do we get choked up when the movies put compassion ahead of profit?

Tuning Up

The play begins with Roger, the punk-rock singer, tuning his guitar. He is having trouble. Mark, the filmmaker, captures this on film. What is Roger doing? "I'm writing one great song – " he says, interrupted by the phone. It is Mark's mother, calling to say we love you, we miss you, sorry your girlfriend Maureen dumped you for another woman. She leaves a message on the answering machine as Mark refuses to pick up the phone to speak with her. When Mark tries again to interview Roger, the phone rings again. Their old roommate Collins is downstairs, and as they speak, Collins is abruptly mugged. A third phone call. It is their ex-roommate Benny who has bought the building and become their landlord; he demands the past year's rent, which Mark and Roger do not have.

Artistic creation connects with human relationships. From the first moment, Larson asks us to consider the tensions within those relationships. He asks us to consider what is constant and what is changing. With Benny's call, we are brought to the question of property. What do Larson's conceptions of artistic creation and human relationships have to teach us about property?

For one thing, Larson focuses on relationships, and human relationships entail obligations as well as rights. In addition, he confronts us with the paradoxes of artistic creation. Surprise can come only if there is a convention to defy. Harmony can be experienced only in relation to dissonance. Stability can be created only if change is also possible. These signs of complexity give us hints about Larson's conception of property.

As we shall see, his notion of property requires us to understand that property derives its power and its justice — as well as its injustice — from the tension between the notion of absolute rights and the notion of rights as contextually dependent, as responsive to human needs as they play out in social life. Larson forces us to see that the notion of property as an absolute right is internally inconsistent and self-defeating. Property is a paradox. It aims at security and stability. Yet this stability can be achieved only by making property rights responsive to each person's need to have some measure of that same security. This requires making property rights contingent on their effects in the world and especially on their effects on those excluded from the world of property.

Torn Apart

When Benny calls to demand the last year's rent, Mark and Roger are shocked. When he bought the building, he suggested that they could stay for free. The very first song confronts the ambiguities in this situation. Do they owe the rent? What do they owe Benny? What does he owe them? Has Benny, the roommate turned landlord, breached an obligation of trust with Mark and Roger? Or have they taken advantage of him?

The first song in the opera, "Rent," calls on the ambiguities in the meaning of the term. Rent means the payments due a landlord. Yet the first song notes another meaning: "torn apart" or "ripping away." Rend is an almost archaic term. The usage that comes to mind is "he rent his clothes," an image of despair and loss that represents grief at the death of a loved one. The phrase comes from Genesis (*Bereishit*) 37:34.[18] It is what Jacob does when he sees Joseph's bloody coat and exclaims: "Joseph is torn, torn-to-pieces."[19] The image is thrust upon us at the moment Collins gets mugged in the opening scene; the muggers take his coat, ripping it off him, ripping it in two. Collins is left with one sleeve on his arm. The image of a rent garment, at the moment Collins meets Angel, a street performer with whom Collins falls in love, foreshadows the death of Angel and Collins' grief. How does the rent owed a landlord relate to grief at the death of a loved one?

In its meaning as rental payment, rent means obligation. In its meaning as "torn apart," rent means a fundamental fracture. Larson asks us to consider how we can "connect" when our relationships with others are broken. The rent concept thus suggests at once connection and isolation, attachment and alienation. Obligations, in turn, can be either legitimate or illegitimate; they can attest to relationships of mutual recognition (you've given me a "new lease on life") or oppression. Rent, as tear, can also evoke either the fact of rupture or the need to repair what is broken. The ambiguity in the situation is manifest: Do Mark and Roger owe the rent or does Benny owe them the right to stay without rent? Benny is their landlord (he owns the building) but also was their roommate – their co-owner – and he was their friend. The relationship – both the landlord-tenant relationship and their friendship – is "torn." Who tore it and why?

The problem of relationship recurs. Even before Benny calls to threaten eviction, we hear a voice message from Mark's mother consoling him because his girlfriend Maureen has left him for another woman, Joanne. Soon we discover that Roger has not left the apartment in six months. He has been in withdrawal from heroin since his girlfriend April committed suicide, leaving a note telling him they both had AIDS. In between these revelations, their friend Tom Collins calls up to their room, gets mugged, and is rescued by Angel. We find out that both Angel and Collins have AIDS, too. We also meet a homeless man who sings about what Christmas Eve means to him: "Christmas bells are ringing/somewhere else! Not here."

In the chaotic first ten minutes of the show, a connection is being made between love and ownership. Love involves relations with others: intimate, inviting, fulfilling, as well as dangerous, fearful, and agonizing. Larson directly relates the problems of two-person relationships, their beginnings and ends, their strengths and vicissitudes, to the relationships among roommates, between landlords and tenants, and between owners and the homeless. Rent as obligation vies with rent as the state of being torn. Something is solid and something is broken in these relationships. There is a failure of connection. Throughout, the metaphor of AIDS is a horrible reminder of the fragility and infinite worth of life, one that echoes the fragility of their tenure in their homes.

The image of rent as the place of the temporary suggests a fundamental instability, and the main response to it is a yearning for security and order. One yearns for life, and for friendship, family, and love. One yearns for a home, a place of connection, a place of safety. As renters, Roger and Mark are vulnerable, a phone call away from being homeless themselves.

Temporariness is a problem, but so is permanence. Permanence, in the form of ownership, provides stability for those who are protected by it, while creating instability and insecurity for those left outside. Property rights may create stability for the owner, but those very same rights are what make the homeless vulnerable. Benny, as owner, can threaten his friends with eviction. He can eject homeless squatters from his lot. His stability is their instability. Moreover, his conception of the prerogatives of ownership seems to block access to the norms associated with friendship, to his social ideals, and to his conscience. He conceives of ownership as the right to be indifferent to nonowners. If he remembers his conscience at all, he imagines that others will respond to the homeless people he will eject. He imagines this, but he has no assurance that it is so. He freeloads on the charity of others.

Permanent, timeless solutions – fixed property rights – do not respond to human needs. If the effects of recognizing fixed property rights are irrelevant – if we are content to have "no safety net" – then "Christmas bells are ringing/somewhere else! Not here." For permanence to be extended to everyone, property rights must be adjusted to ensure a fair distribution of stability and instability.

In the rent image, Larson suggests a middle course between complete permanence (fixed ownership rights without obligation) and complete vulnerability (homelessness). He asks us to look at relationships, with their obligations, as well as their claims on us. He proposes a new model of property along with a new model of life – a way to cope in a life that has been rendered vulnerable both by AIDS and by the withdrawal of the safety net. Rent, in other words, describes both a problem and a path toward a solution.

Life Support

After early revelations that Roger, Collins, and Angel have AIDS, we are taken to an AIDS support group. This support group sings a "credo." This is all there is; live today as if it were the only day. You are not dying from AIDS, you are living with it. Choose life, and choose it now. The support group and the credo are the central images of the play, nourishing both the individuals living with AIDS and the couples who break up and reunite. In the end, the support group furnishes the most powerful image of several strategies for dealing with the problem of homelessness.

The AIDS support group sings the credo while standing in a circle. They sing it together, as a chorale or a hymn. It is hopeful; it is life affirming. And a hymn that is called a credo invokes the presence of God. But soon after the group breaks up, the members sing another song, a song composed only of questions, a song of despair. "Will I lose my dignity?" they ask. "Will anyone care?" The credo is forgotten; this is a nightmare and they are terrified. And the most terrifying thing of all is the fear that they have no one to turn to. If, in America, at the end of the millennium, "you are what you own," does this mean you are on your own? Their greatest fear, their greatest question: Am I alone? There is no hope in these questions. And they are not answered.

Yet an answer glimmers in the musical form that the questions take. It is a round – a musical circle that parallels the physical circle in which they stood as they sang the credo. Each of the individuals asks the same questions, and, in the make-believe world of the stage, they do it together, musically. One imagines people gathered in a place of worship, asking questions that have no answer. Why do bad things happen to good people?[20] They get spiritual support, but not because their questions are answered. God may be present, but God is also silent. They get support from the fact that they are there, asking the questions together, standing in the presence of God.

A recently composed piece of chamber music by Andrew Imbrie was written after the death of the composer's son. Onstage is a wind quintet, representing life. Offstage is a string quartet. The music offstage is ethereal, beautiful, and it never changes. Onstage, where life takes place, the music is excited, happy, intricate. And then things go wrong; the son dies and the music becomes agonized and dissonant. Offstage, the string quartet keeps playing, unchanged in any way. There is no response to the travails occurring on stage. Eventually, the music onstage calms down, but it never returns to the happy, uncomplicated music that began the piece.

In one reading, the string quartet represents a distant and uninvolved God, a God who allowed the Holocaust to occur, who allowed young people to become infected by the AIDS virus and die before their time. Despair and grief reign in the world, and God is oblivious. On another reading, the music offstage never stops; it never wavers; it never fails. It is steady, peaceful, present, neither loud nor soft, just very, very present. No matter what happens onstage, the quartet remains there, calm, supportive.

The repeated despairing questions asked by the members of the support group suggest a model of support that does not come from having a simple answer. The voices overlap. The second voice metaphorically *leans* on the first voice, as the second singer literally *leans* on the first singer. They imbricate each other.[21] They are separate and yet intimately involved. The round form suggests a means of obtaining support and meaning in the face of unmitigated doubt. The individual is not obliterated; individual voices remain. Yet, at the same time, they are not fully independent; they overlap, they lean on each other, each one with a hand on the shoulder of the one next to her. Connection is simultaneously with the one next to you and with the group as a whole, facing inward to the circle, seeing every other one asking the same questions. They are individuals, but they are not alone.

You Are What You Own

In different ways, Roger and Mark are tempted by selfishness. Roger flees from Mimi because he cannot bear to watch her die. Mark is tempted by a job offer from a sleazy television show. Yet they both reject selfishness. They reject Benny's offer to give them a rent-free apartment and a cyber-arts studio in return for persuading Maureen to give up her protest. Roger returns to Mimi, just as Mark decides not to "sell out" or choose his work based solely on what the market will bear. They learn what is important. They seek love; they seek meaning.

Benny believes that he is promoting the public good, that the neighborhood will be better off if he develops the vacant lot. This mantra is familiar to us. But something else is familiar as well. He is indifferent to the fate of the people he will evict. They are a necessary cost of progress.

This is the image of justice presented by Thrasymachus in Plato's *Republic* as interpreted by Elizabeth V. Spelman. Benny wants Roger and Mark to understand and accept that their happiness is contingent on the grief of others; the suffering of others is a necessary cost of their own success. But Roger and Mark reject this offer. They are unwilling to consider their own success to be inextricably tied to the loss of others. They reject the view of Thrasymachus (and Benny) that "the misery of other people doesn't touch us." They cannot "take pleasure in performing actions that [they] know to cause great misery in others." Rather, like Socrates, they see their "happiness as compatible with the happiness of others, and . . . other people's misery as affecting the possibility of [their] own."[22] They are unwilling to pursue their goals in this way, if it has these effects on others who are even more vulnerable than they.

As they choose to connect with others, they convert the theme of "dying in America" to a quest for life; dying from AIDS becomes living with AIDS. "You are what you own" becomes a call to "come into our own." And what does it mean to come into our own? It means "connection – in an isolating age." It means you are not alone. What most sustains them is not "ownership" but their connection with each other. They are human because they are not alone. They are human because they are not willing to treat other human beings as if they were necessary costs of progress.

"You are what you own" is both the problem and the solution. If you are what you own, each person must own something so that they can be, so that they can come into their own.

The tension is manifest. Property is a paradox. Its purpose is security, autonomy, and control. Every person is a monarch of his or her castle, with a room of one's own to make a life and to create a world. Yet this control depends on the right to exclude, the very right that may sometimes deny autonomy to others. The consequence of property as exclusion may be the exclusion of others from the realm of dignity, of property. The institution of private property presupposes that it is potentially available to all. Yet the very recognition of property rights in owners entails the ability to control scarce resources needed to sustain human life.[23] The exclusionary nature of property means that the extent of owners' property rights can be legitimately defined only by ensuring that those rights do not result in the exclusion of others from access to property for themselves. The absolute conception of the property right is self-contradictory. Property rights depend on, and cannot exist without, the ability to bear this tension, to regulate it, to recognize it, to affirm it.

Larson presents the AIDS support group as a metaphor for the social aspect of the institution of property. The group stands in a circle and affirms the preciousness of life, of *each life,* each person present. Even in the face of unmitigated despair, the round form suggests a way to construct a circle that recognizes the dilemmas of each individual life while allowing each one to lean on others. The circle possesses entitlement and a forward motion, a sustaining quality. Just as the voices in the round lean on each other while retaining their individuality, property owners have obligations as well as rights. Each one facing into the circle, while finding a place to stand, suggests a way to live with the tension between the individual and the community. Individuals stand in relation to others, each voice important, crucial for the maintenance of the musical energy.

Property is conceptualized, in Larson's world, not as plots with owners possessing absolute rights, but owners situated in relation to others with a combination of rights and obligations. Indeed, their property gets its value, not just because of their individual efforts, but because of its place in a social system. Each owner depends on the efforts of the others, as well as her own. Just as the voices of the round overlap, so do property rights. Property rights entail obligations to respect the rights of others. This mutual regard does not mean that each has the right to be relentlessly selfish. Rather, it means that individuals must ensure that their property rights do not have the effect of denying minimal standards of human decency to others.

The widespread admiration for Aaron Feuerstein suggests that the absolute notion of ownership – with the shareholders conceptualized as "owners" of the corporation and the workers as expendable "factors of production" – denies not only the workers' dignity and security but their ability to become owners. Real protection for property rights would ensure that the workers would not be cast out of the system in a way that prevents them from achieving the stability associated with ownership rather than dependence. People do adjust over time; they get new jobs, they move on. But some people do not. The policies that would work well in these transitional settings are hard to define. Nonetheless, an attitude of indifference to the suffering of those who are the victims of change, who are excluded from property by the claimed rights of the owner, and who have no reasonable alternative, goes against our cultural narrative, as Larson saw.

Our brave new world of self-reliance makes everyone vulnerable. The ultimate lesson of *Rent* is the need for "connection – in an isolating age." As Christian activist Jim Wallis notes, "We need to find and feel a connection to one another."[24] These insights have consequences for the ways we shape our relationship to property.

CHAPTER FIVE

Common Decency

If economic policy-making does not acknowledge the complex-ities of the inner moral life of each human being, its strivings and perplexities, its complicated emotions, its efforts at under-standing and its terror, if it does not distinguish in its descrip-tions between a human life and a machine, then we should re-gard with suspicion its claim to govern a nation of human beings; and we should ask ourselves whether, having seen us as little different from inanimate objects, it might not be capable of treating us with a certain obtuseness.[1]

— Martha Nussbaum, *Poetic Justice*

Human beings need all the relatives they can get — as possible donors or receivers not necessarily of love, but of common de-cency.[2]

— Kurt Vonnegut, *Slapstick*

Individual property interests derive their value partly because the legal system requires each actor to take some account of the interests of oth-ers and of the environment in which we live. That environment is a common asset and it includes human as well as natural resources. The extent, distribution, and character of property rights are determined by moral, religious, and legal regulatory systems that enjoin each of us to moderate selfishness with attention to the common good.

Both conservatives and liberals should be concerned about imple-menting public policies designed to ensure that everyone can obtain property. Widespread distribution of property would promote values that are treasured by both left and right. The left should want this be-cause it would promote both equality and individual liberty, giving families a material base from which to exercise free choice about private life. The right should want this because a home and a stable job provide the means for promoting family values and strong communities.

What general principles would govern a just economy? People who can work, either outside or inside the home, should be able to do so and to obtain a living wage. Everyone who can work should be able to get a job and should be able to earn enough to attain a decent livelihood. It should be possible for everyone to take care of themselves and their families and obtain the minimum necessary for a dignified human life. People who cannot work should be entitled to live in dignity. In this regard, it is crucial that our institutions ensure that children are cared for and that the work of taking care of children or adults who need caretaking is both socially recognized and economically compensated. We need to wrestle with the problems of establishing just ground rules that will enable employees to keep work on fair terms once they get it, to participate in governing their work lives, to obtain a desirable balance between stability and flexibility, to be able to combine work and family life, and to obtain transitional assistance in the face of economic change.

None of these principles is easy to implement in practice. There are myriad ways to achieve these goals, and some may interfere with others. Humility is required and attention to the real-world consequences of different strategies is crucial. Nonetheless, it is imperative that we work to achieve both material prosperity *and* social justice. Neither is meaningful without the other and there is no reason to believe we need to trade off one for the other. *We can do good and do well at the same time.*

Property and Social Connections

We do not live alone. Yet we sometimes act as if we did. When we enter the world of the marketplace, in particular, we may feel entitled to pursue our own interests and ignore the needs of others. Business owners try to maximize profits. Corporate managers both feel morally obligated and are legally obligated to do so on behalf of shareholders. In the service of these ends, they may adopt strategies that have untold human costs. They may lay off thousands of workers, disrupting the lives of both individuals and communities. Workers may similarly seek their own interests rather than the interests of the corporate enterprise or the community. In defense of their own economic interests, workers may engage in slowdowns or go out on strike, intending to pressure the employer by inconveniencing the public. They may have a just cause, but the struggle is not without its human costs. When we enter the world of politics, we see similar expressions of self-interest at the expense of community needs. Business groups lobby Congress for repeal or limitation of socially desirable environmental laws. Hard-working taxpayers support elimination of welfare on the ground that those who work should not have to subsidize those who do not.

When we are thinking religiously or ethically, however, we recognize both personal responsibilities and obligations to others. We give money and assistance to charities. We help our friends, coworkers, and neighbors in times of family tragedies and natural disasters. Such instances of fellow feeling are not limited to extraordinary situations, however. We can discern a good deal of evidence of individual and collective commitment to be responsive to the needs of others.

At the same time, we tend to segregate self-interest and obligation. In the world of the market, we valorize the pursuit of happiness and we try to satisfy the immediate preferences of individuals, whatever they happen to be. This is the world of profit. In the world of the family, friendship, charitable giving, and religious life, we valorize compassion, fellow feeling, and attentiveness to the needs of others, especially the most vulnerable among us. This is the world of compassion.

We seem eager to separate the world of profit and the world of compassion. But these worlds have never been and cannot be fully separate. Consider the role of government and law. On one hand, we might consider this to be part of the world of profit. After all, people lobby for laws that promote their interests. On the other hand, governance is a central arena where we consider the public interest. We pass laws not only to promote the self-interest of constituent groups but also to promote justice. Antidiscrimination and environmental laws, for example, function partly to protect the self-interest of those benefited by them, but they are primarily intended to serve a notion of the greater good. Many laws promulgate minimum standards for a variety of social activities. Building codes protect individuals from shoddy or dangerous construction. Zoning laws promote safe and pleasant environments and facilitate the creation of particular types of neighborhoods.

Politics is constituted not only by clashes among interest groups and the appeals of lobbyists, but by a sense of justice, the public good, the common wealth. Politics is moved by ideals as well as by self-interest. The contest among political parties is necessarily a contest of social visions, of conceptions of the good society. Self-interest is also present in politics but is pursued in a context of persuasion and justification that claims that public policy must respond to public norms such as liberty, equality, fairness, democracy, and individual dignity.

Law mediates between the world of profit and the world of compassion. It does so not by separating them into separate spheres, but by creating a political and economic regime that reflects a mixture of ideals. Surprising as it may seem, even the world of profit is infused with the world of compassion. The law has always recognized obligations of fairness and decency in market relationships. It is true that this recognition has waxed and waned with time, but it has always been there. The law has also always imposed obligations on owners to use their property with a view toward protecting other owners and the legitimate interests of the community.

In recent years, the rhetoric of profit has eclipsed the rhetoric of compassion. We have come close to banning the rhetoric of compassion in the public worlds of the market, politics, and the law. Those who speak publicly about compassion are ridiculed as liberals who do not understand the way the world works. The ideology of selfishness and absolute property rights is prevalent, yet it is distorted and false. It is not true to our own deepest beliefs; it is a false representation both of our most cherished values and our actual laws and institutions. I do not mean that self-reliance and liberty are not *parts* of our moral and legal universe; I mean that they are not the *whole*. Treated as the whole, they are both morally pernicious and self-defeating.

The ideology of selfishness is both a poor description of what we value and a moral nightmare. Those in public life who present this ideology to us pretend that their ideals of liberty and property will solve all evils. But absolute liberty and absolute property rights represent a view we do not accept. Not even the most fanatical libertarian actually accepts the idea that we are totally on our own, that government is wholly pernicious, that liberty and property have no limits. In fact, the very institution of property requires extensive regulation to assign, protect, and adjudicate conflicts among property rights. Rather, the key question is what norms we should use in determining what we will make property mean.

"We are living in a money culture," wrote John Dewey in 1930. "Its cult and rites dominate." We reward those who are successful in the production of value. But what values count? If one looks at our economic system, Dewey said, we see a culture divided into two classes, the haves and the have-nots. Most Americans justified this division, Dewey argued, because they believed that American life offers "unparalleled opportunities for each individual to prosper according to his virtues." If one were trying to guess the values of such a society, one might suppose that the supreme value would be the production and earning of wealth. This "would seem to imply a pretty definitely materialistic scheme of value."[3]

This system produces great wealth for some and insecurity for others. "If the mass of workers live in constant fear of loss of their jobs," Dewey noted, "this is doubtless because our spirit of progress . . . keeps everything on the move." The insecurity and inequality this system engenders are "treated as an inevitable part of our social system."[4] Any attempts to use government power to alleviate the rough edges of our economic system are viewed as counterproductive or futile. Celebration of the market appears to suggest that we are in the grip of economic forces we cannot control. Ironically, this view reeks of economic determinism. It is reminiscent of discredited philosophy about inevitable stages of capitalism more than of philosophies that emphasize the role of human agency in history and social life and the importance and dignity of the individual.

What is worse still, Dewey argued, is that this view of economic life "calls for a hard and strenuous philosophy." It would seem that a society that embraced this form of life would glorify the idea of the "struggle for existence and the survival of the economically fit." [5]

> One would expect the current theory of life, if it reflects the actual situation, to be the most drastic Darwinism. And, finally, one would anticipate that the personal traits most prized would be clear-sighted vision of personal advantage and resolute ambition to secure it at any human cost. Sentiment and sympathy would be at the lowest discount. [6]

Yet, strangely, Dewey concluded, we observe nothing of the sort. We observe idealism, not materialism. We "praise even our most successful men, not for their ruthless and self-centered energy in getting ahead, but because of their love of flowers, children, dogs, or their kindness to aged relatives. Anyone who frankly urges a selfish creed of life is everywhere frowned upon." [7] There is a strange contradiction, Dewey contended, in our culture.

Joseph Weintraub, a former chief justice of the Supreme Court of New Jersey, wrote, "Property rights serve human values. They are recognized to that end, and are limited by it." [8] Our religious traditions support compassion and mutual support. But surprisingly, our legal tradition is not so different. The world of profit and the world of compassion meet at the intersection of law. The ideals of law are ideals about the just contours of social life. This poses a question for us. What kinds of social relationships should the law encourage and which should it preclude? What values should inform public policy?

Richard Sennett notes that when he interviewed managers who had laid off workers, they became "acutely and personally uncomfortable, fidgeting or breaking eye contact or retreating into taking notes, if forced to discuss the people who, in their jargon, are 'left behind.'" [9]

It is good that such managers feel discomfort; they are responding, as Jean-Jacques Rousseau says, to the "first promptings of humanity."[10] The question is whether we can construct a society in which those "left behind" through no fault of their own still might have a way to catch up. Can we find a way to balance the bottom line and the human heart?

Sociologist Katherine Newman has shown that people in the United States tend to understand economic failure as personal. They believe that those who make it deserve to make it, for the most part, and that those who fail do so because of some personal deficiency.[11] This is the case even when it is clear to an objective observer that the failure involved not any personal inability to perform, but systemic factors beyond the control of those who failed. We would like to believe that our economic system rewards the deserving and that there is sufficient opportunity for those left behind to re-enter the system, to contribute, and to make a living. But the reality is that many people face difficulties not of their own making. Businesses fail even though talented employees worked hard. Jobs paying minimum wage do not provide enough income to pay for decent housing, food, clothing, transportation, child care, and medical care. Increasing global competition and changes in corporate culture produce great instability in the job market.

Property protects security and provides a chance to participate in economic and social life. The have-nots, as much as the haves, are entitled to the benefits property provides. Property is not only about ownership; it is about affording access to ownership. No one can be left out. I take this as a premise. It makes little difference if one bases it on the Lockean notion of the importance of individual dignity or the religious notion that each human being is created in the image of God. If everyone must be included, then the law governing economic and social life must make it possible – really possible – for individuals to find their place in the world and to make it.

Property reflects our social connections. To the extent that people think that there is something about property, as an entitlement or an institution, that prevents us from acting on our compassionate impulses, they are mistaken. Property is something we must collectively define and construct. The tensions that inform property are the tensions inherent in social relationships. There is no way to manage a property system without making value choices. We have values other than self-interest that govern our interactions with others. Those values are crucial in determining the legitimate meaning and scope of property rights. The law is the site where those values are effectuated and implemented. Property is not just about self-interest. It is about creating the ground rules for fair social relationships.

The ideals that justify the institution of property press in the direction of ensuring that access to ownership is both widely dispersed and universally available. Property, as a legal and social institution, requires us to take the interests of others into account even when they control things that we need. This is an extraordinary thing to ask of someone. We ask nonowners to respect the interests of owners; we ask the have-nots to defer to the haves. The question is why property owners should not have the same obligation – to take the interests of others into account. Asking the haves to respect the interests of the have-nots seems less of a burden than asking the have-nots to respect the interests of the haves. The least we can do is to ensure that the legal and economic systems are sufficiently permeable so that the have-nots can become haves. If each person is of equal importance and equally entitled to a dignified life, then a just property system is as much about getting property as it is about keeping it.

Do we owe each other anything? Do moral obligations have any place in the business world or in the law governing market relationships? The answer to both questions is a resounding yes. The ethics of the marketplace, of course, are not identical to the ethics of other spheres of life, such as friendship, but the market is not the place for relentless self-interest, as some suspect and others hope. Just as the world of sports values good sportsmanship, so too is the world of economic relationships characterized by rules designed to create a fair playing field.

This insight has two implications. First, we should want business executives, and others in positions of responsibility and power, to exercise good judgment. We should like them to act wisely. They should be able to be proud of what they do and how they conduct themselves. This means that we should not ask or expect our businesspeople to make a profit at any cost or in any way.

We should expect every person, in their daily lives, to pay attention to norms of conduct that accord with their considered judgments about what, all things considered, is the right thing to do. Lawyers and businesspeople, employers and employees, professionals and clients, managers and workers – all should strive to act with practical wisdom. We should not check our morality at the factory gates or at the boardroom door. Asking market participants to act wisely requires changes in culture, but it also requires changes in law. At the very least, the law should allow and ideally should encourage and sometimes mandate that people act in their day-to-day lives in ways that we would, at the end of the day, find admirable.

Of course, we do not all agree about which acts are admirable and which are dreadful, which are right and which are wrong. This is often taken as a reason for separating morality from the worlds of business and law. I take the opposite lesson. I would like to have discussions in corporate boardrooms, in law firms, on the shop floor and the union hall, that revolve around the question, "Is it the right thing to do?"

The second implication of the necessary link between morality and economic life is that the rules governing the acquisition and use of property do or should reflect our need to temper pursuit of profit and wealth with the desire for right conduct and social justice. At a minimum, this means that we must not only allow each person to enter the system on fair terms, but must also ensure that those who cannot work are guaranteed access to the means necessary for a dignified human life. The rules of the game are established, to a very large extent, by law, and it has never been the case that the law governing the market has allowed individuals to act without regard to the consequences of their actions for other people. Property law has never given owners rights without also giving them responsibilities. One of those fundamental responsibilities is the obligation to ensure that access to the system is available to all.

Getting Work

We are beginning to feel the effects of welfare reform. Public reaction is surprisingly ambivalent. Although extremely popular, the implementation of welfare reform has raised disturbing questions. In the Commonwealth of Massachusetts, for example, welfare benefits were due to end for many families on December 1, 1998. As that date approached, public authorities announced that they would delay benefit cutoffs for most families until after Christmas. Although state officials explained that the delay reflected bureaucratic difficulties in implementing the cutoff, it was widely believed that the delay also had something to do with uneasiness about public reaction to the timing of the cutoffs. It seemed callous to cut off benefits just before Christmas.

Whatever the reason for the delay, the timing of the planned cutoffs struck many people as problematic. The spirit of the Christmas season led them to question the human effects of what the state was about to do. And yet, one wonders, if it would be callous to cut benefits at Christmastime, why does it suddenly become acceptable and even advisable to do so a month later?

Derrick Jackson reports that welfare reform is generally viewed as a phenomenal success. In an editorial in the *Boston Globe,* he wrote:

Wisconsin, one of the most aggressive states in driving the poor off the rolls, released data that found that 62 percent of recipients who left welfare in early 1998 still had jobs by last fall. This prompted welfare guru Larry Mead of New York University to say: "These work levels represent the greatest achievement in antipoverty policy since the Great Society."

That must be easy for him to say, since Mead is obviously not one of the 38 percent of former welfare recipients who is *un*employed. It is amazing in an America that is supposedly in the midst of a boom, that 4 out of 10 people in a given group are unemployed and this is hailed as a major social victory.[12]

People are off the rolls, voluntarily or involuntarily. What they find, out there in the world, is both opportunity and danger. The base requirement for social justice in the post–welfare-reform state is access to a job. Yet, despite the low overall unemployment rate, many are not able to find jobs.[13] It is cruel to cut people from support on the supposition that they can work if no one will hire them.

Some economists explain the increasing inequality of income in terms of technological change. Although education is obviously an important factor in rising out of poverty, I am skeptical of the view that education alone will solve these problems. While it is true that some workers are not educated even for the jobs of the twentieth century (adult illiteracy is a serious problem), giving everyone a good education will not, by itself, ensure that everyone can get a job. It may simply increase competition for the jobs that exist. Nonetheless, it is true that part of the problem could be solved by improving our education system and making adult education available for those who need it, either to catch up or to be retrained for the new jobs of the twenty-first century.

Educational policy is obviously sensitive and complicated. A simple change in attitudes about the *amount* of education we should expect to be available might be helpful. For example, we might start public schools at age three rather than five or six, to give all parents the ability to find, and the option to use, high-quality day care. More and more families find that they cannot live on one salary and such day care is becoming a necessity; it clearly is so for those who have been thrown off welfare. Such preschool education will not only prepare children to learn and allow them to acquire social skills, but will also make it possible for parents who cannot afford private day care to get the benefits available to others.

On the other end of the educational pathway, we might work to ensure every adult twenty or more years of guaranteed education.

Thirteen of those years would be encompassed by kindergarten to high school graduation (fifteen if public schools started at age three). Four more would allow one to go to college. A twenty or twenty-two year entitlement would allow people to receive adult education later in life, perhaps at a time when they need retraining for a new or different kind of job.

Education appears to be essential, but it is not enough. If we want strong communities, we need policies that will create jobs in areas of high unemployment. Enterprise zones are one response to this problem, but they have not been sufficient. It might be possible to increase the availability of tax credits for employers who hire welfare recipients or who relocate to economically depressed areas, or take other action to create jobs in depressed areas. Current policies are clearly not working.

All of this may still not be enough. Some workers with low skills will simply not be hired by the private sector. If we are not going to have general assistance or welfare anymore, then it is imperative to insure that *some* job is available to everyone who can work. For this reason, the government should be the employer of last resort. The Works Progress Administration (WPA) employed thousands of people in the Depression years and was responsible for rebuilding hundreds of public buildings, roads, airports, and bridges. It also provided work for writers, artists, and musicians. [14] We have similar unmet needs now for public infrastructure, education, and child care. In addition, government hiring at fair wages can place some pressure on private business to increase salaries in order to compete for workers.

It is obviously problematic to ask the government to be the employer of last resort. It may be hard to match individuals to jobs. Poorly managed systems may rely on jobs that may be make-work and on dead-end jobs that will neither promote dignity nor lift a family out of poverty. Nonetheless, as the WPA demonstrates, it is possible to design a system that would work well. More importantly, it is cruel to base public policy on the assumption that everyone can find a job if this is not the case. I do not pretend that any of this would be easy or inexpensive. I am asking us to confront the fact that the value Americans place on self-sufficiency only makes moral sense if it is possible to act on those expectations. Job creation for those left out of the system should be a major moral priority.

A Living Wage

It is apparent that the amount one can earn on the minimum wage is not sufficient to enable a single, working parent to raise a family out of poverty. A person who worked forty hours per week at $5.25 an hour for fifty weeks would have a yearly income of $10,500. This amount is not sufficient to pay for food, housing, medical care, transportation, clothing, and child care – to say nothing of other things most of us take for granted, such as a toy for a child, dinner at a restaurant, an occasional trip to a museum or a movie theater. John E. Schwarz notes that "in 1994 the American public responded to the Roper poll that it took a family of four about $25,000 just to get by; the federal poverty line for a family of four for that year stood at about $15,000." Moreover, Schwarz argues that not enough good jobs exist to enable families to obtain a minimally decent lifestyle. He estimates that the shortage of good jobs leaves roughly 15.7 million households out in the cold. [15]

Low-wage workers face huge obstacles to earning enough money. Many find only part-time jobs or jobs that do not have benefits such as health insurance. Others cannot find jobs that they can coordinate with available child care. One-third of all poor children live in families whose parents work. [16] A recent study of families forced off welfare in Massachusetts found that only 75 percent of the former recipients were working, and most of those had already held low-paying jobs while on welfare. Although the parents were earning more than they had on welfare, their average earnings were less than $9,300 per year, far below the federal poverty level of $13,650 for a family of three. [17]

Most welfare recipients always used welfare as a form of temporary transitional assistance between jobs or after a divorce. A small minority were on welfare for long periods of time. The overwhelming majority were on welfare for less than two years. This suggested to some policy makers that welfare could be turned into a short-term matter and that there are jobs for all who are willing to work. Cutting benefits after two years or so is said to be necessary to give the few who stayed on welfare a push to get out and work, as others do.

The problem is that aggregate statistics do not tell us about the situation of individuals. Nor do they tell us about the distribution of opportunities and vulnerabilities. Are available jobs located where welfare recipients live? There are indications that they are not. Do available jobs, for which people are qualified, pay high enough wages to sustain a family with children? There are substantial indications that, for many people in many places, the answer is no. Are there individuals who, for whatever reason, are not likely to be able to obtain jobs even when their welfare benefits are cut off? It is clear that the answer is yes.

If we care about alleviating poverty, promoting dignity, and protecting the well-being of children, it is apparent that more has to be done. It is not acceptable to push people off welfare on the theory that they can work when there are no jobs for them to take. It is not acceptable to force people to live on the minimum wage and to cut off medical care, food stamps, and housing allowances if the wages they earn are not sufficient to sustain a family. It is not acceptable for children to come to school hungry, without winter coats, and to be left at home alone after school while their parents work.[18]

We have adopted a variety of strategies to deal with these problems. Many of them are helpful. They include, for example, a mandated minimum wage and the earned income tax credit (EITC) that either reduces taxes paid by the poor or supplements their wages to raise family income to above the poverty level. We have provided private employers with subsidies to induce them to hire certain disadvantaged potential employees, such as young people, welfare recipients, and veterans.[19] We have increased enforcement of child support obligations on fathers.

These steps are starts. But the rate of poverty among children, just as one of many indications, indicts even these steps as inadequate. We need to reduce red tape, increase funding, and target amounts so that individuals have financial incentives to work and so that they are able to obtain a minimally decent standard of living for themselves and their children if they do work. We might also deduct child support payments from paychecks the way we deduct social security payments. This might equalize the pressure on fathers and mothers to care for their children. Child care is subsidized to allow some poor parents to afford quality child care when they are working. Housing assistance is available through publicly provided housing or through the section 8 program, in which the government pays a portion of a tenant's rent directly to the private landlord, allowing some of the poor to afford housing. The problem is that these programs are not sufficient.[20] The minimum wage does not bring a family out of poverty and in many cases, it does not do so even when combined with the EITC. The average wait to get a section 8 voucher is twenty-eight months.[21]

Perhaps most important, none of these programs faces the fact that some subset of welfare recipients is simply not employable. They may be unemployable because they have disabilities. Or they may face medical problems, including drug and alcohol addiction and depression. They may have inadequate education or training or work experience, such that no employer would feel ready to offer them an entry-level job. They may be victims of domestic violence or be responsible for the care of other people's children. They may live far from available jobs.

It is certainly true that there were serious problems with the welfare system before the current round of welfare reform. But it is also true that some aspects of welfare reform are likely to increase, rather than decrease, both poverty and human suffering. Policy makers need to consider a combination of policies, such as raising the minimum wage and the EITC, improving child support enforcement, granting additional assistance for those who have trouble mixing the heavy demands of child care and work outside the home, and easing requirements for disability benefits so that those who are not able to care for themselves are not left in desperation.

As with the problem of job creation, the problem of making sure that work pays enough to raise people and their families out of poverty is an extremely complicated one. Some incentives backfire. Some things don't work out as we plan. Sometimes one policy may work at cross-purposes with another. It is not acceptable, however, to place the burden squarely on those who are most vulnerable to work these problems out for themselves.

Caretaking

Millions of people take care of others, and most of them do it for free. A large number of these are parents taking care of children. And most of those doing the caretaking are women. A growing number are grandmothers caring for grandchildren. This trend has been exacerbated by welfare reform; when mothers are unable or unwilling to work, the grandmothers are often pressed into service to take care of the children.[22] Many adults take care of their parents or other relatives, especially those with disabilities or those who are sick or troubled. This work is essential to those who need it and is often central to the identity of those who provide it. It is socially valuable labor; it is necessary work, although it is often a labor of love. It must be done, and though it is unpaid, it is not free. Someone must take care of the caretakers.

Conservatives as well as liberals consider mothers and fathers to be "working" when they are home mothering and fathering. Yet, strangely, conservatives do not consider mothers to be working if they have no spouse providing an income for the family. We hear that welfare mothers must "work." This is premised on the notion that the work they do at home – taking care of their children – is not work.[23]

We could have gotten rid of welfare simply by thinking of public assistance to families with dependent children as a salary paid to individuals working in the field of child care. Such a salary would be paid in the absence of any other family income earned by a spouse or other family member employed in the private or public sector. "Family allowances" are common, for example, in Europe.[24] Although some fathers perform child care, it is still the case that mothers provide most of it. This uncompensated work is a major reason for the continued relative poverty of both women and children in the United States.

If we were serious about valuing the work that parents do, we might seriously consider an allowance for every person who is taking care of another person. Instead, we provided "family allowances" only to those who needed it. The effect of making public aid to families with children dependent on need was that being a "welfare mother" became a stigma. This is a chronic problem. If we press for economic benefits for all who take care of children, we may have trouble obtaining public support since money would go to some individuals who do not need it. If, instead, we make the payments need based, we stigmatize those who receive it and act against current political realities which do not seem to consider child care a form of work or personal responsibility.

Rather than adopt a policy of giving economic value to those who perform the socially useful work of taking care of dependent children and others, we have adopted a policy of forcing poor mothers to work outside, as well as inside, the home. Who will take care of the children? Consider this story from the *New York Times:*

> The [welfare mother] had signed an agreement with the state to go to college, which she believed offered her the best route to a job that paid enough to support her three children. She was put on a waiting list. Her caseworker told her she would have to get a job in the meantime. A few weeks after she began working for $5.50 an hour, her 5-year-old got sick. The boy was running a fever and could not go to the day-care center. The worker then told the mother that the only acceptable excuse for missing work was a doctor's note saying that she herself was ill. So she left her son with a neighbor. When she came home, she found him alone and untended. She stayed home with him and was fired from her job. Her welfare benefits were then reduced because she had not done what her worker required. Unable to pay the rent, the family was evicted . . . and slept in a friend's car. Because of the fam-

ily homelessness, one of the children's teachers reported them to child-protection services. The child-protection worker told the mother that her children would be placed in foster care if she could not provide for them.[25]

If the "working" mother earns enough to pay for the needs of her family, she could provide and care for them. Yet it is apparent that the low wages earned by many "welfare mothers" cannot sustain them and their children. If the minimum wage and the EITC are not sufficient to enable the working parent to pay for housing, clothing, medical care, transportation, and child care, or if child care is not available at the hours when the parent must be at work, or if the quality of the child care is inadequate, then the government must ensure that the children are cared for adequately.[26] This can be accomplished in a variety of ways: by increasing the minimum wage and/or the EITC making sure those entitled to the EITC take advantage of it, subsidizing the creation of jobs where people live and need employment, or creating public jobs that include child care. It is cruelty of the highest order to insist that mothers take care of their children, but then to leave them in a situation where nothing they can do will give their children adequate care. It is imperative that policies be instituted that ensure the availability of affordable, high-quality child care when working parents need it. Problems are especially difficult for poor parents who work at night and on weekends, and for parents of older children, when their children do not qualify for most child care programs and are increasingly left alone at home after school while the parents work.

I have no illusions that it will be easy to develop programs that will give the right incentives, prevent fraud, combat dependency, while taking care of children and making sure that parents have enough time and energy to play with them and read to them, as well as providing them with food and clothes and a safe place to sleep. We need, however, to take the welfare of children as seriously as we take the national defense. This means creating the institutions necessary to balance work and home life, and ensuring the availability of quality child care. It also means creating appropriate incentives to work and to keep families together, and promoting child support by fathers without forcing mothers to remain in abusive relationships. The complexities of responding to the needs of families in crisis are mind-boggling. Throwing people off welfare and hoping they will muddle through is a policy that is bound to fail and to harm the most vulnerable among us.

Keeping Work

Many people used to keep their jobs for a lifetime. Even those with a high school degree or less were able to obtain stable employment. This has become increasingly uncommon. Job stability is becoming a rare commodity. I think job security is a good idea, but this practice has come under attack in recent years. Even the remaining bastions of job tenure, such as the academy and the judiciary, have faced strong challenges to this practice. This is odd, given that tenure is, of course, a kind of property. With the recent expansion of the copyright laws to allow an additional twenty years of protection for intellectual property, and the granting of patents for human genes and other new forms of property, one would have thought that other expansions of the forms of property might be popular with those who wax eloquent about the benefits of private property. Of course, the creation of property rights in jobs does limit freedom of contract by regulating the terms of contractual relationships. It gives employees more than they could otherwise obtain in the marketplace and does so by limiting the property rights of the employer.

We protect property to give security to those who are vulnerable to dispossession. Those who invest their labor deserve security as much as those who invest their money. For that reason, employees deserve some guarantee of continued employment or help in finding new employment if they lose their jobs. They deserve this for precisely the same reasons we protect the property rights of owners. In other words, the very reason we protect property rights in the first place is the reason why we should institute legal reforms to help employees obtain the kind of stability associated with ownership. This should lead us to the task of constructing laws and public policies designed to protect the ability of *everyone* to obtain the kind of security associated with ownership.

We should figure out ways to provide at least as much protection for those who are most vulnerable to the vicissitudes of economic change as we do for those who are its greatest beneficiaries. Our current laws fail in this regard. We encourage employers to treat employees as disposable means of production. Human beings are ends, not means. I do not mean to argue that jobs should be held for life or that we should get rid of the desirable flexibility of a capitalist system. But if we cannot go back to the culture of job security that we once had, we must figure out what institutional structures could replace it, so that we do not lose completely the stability that job security afforded to individuals, their families, and the community.

It is apparent that returning to the situation in which many employees could expect a lifelong association with one company is no longer in the cards. This does not mean, however, that there are no alternatives. We should create incentives (such as favorable tax treatment) to encourage companies again to treat their employees as assets rather than as cuttable costs. We should give employees new ways to make up for the customary job security that now seems to be gone.

For one thing, employers should not be able to mislead workers about the condition of the company or their role in it. Employers sometimes mislead employees through assurances that hard work will be rewarded by a future in the company when the employer, in fact, has no intention of establishing a long-term relationship. As I noted earlier, securities laws require companies to tell existing and potential investors the truth – even to the extent of forcing companies to reveal any material information a prudent investor would need to determine whether to entrust her money to the corporate managers.[27] The protections granted investors should be extended to workers.

A second way to ensure that corporate decision making considers employees' interests in continued employment is to acknowledge that values other than profit maximization should be, not only relevant, but sometimes controlling, in such decision making.[28] This requires some changes in existing law. Again, Feuerstein was able to act as he did because he was the owner of his company. Corporate law requires managers of companies to act in the interests of the shareholders. It has traditionally been understood that their interest is maximization of profit. Feuerstein could have argued that paying his workers' salaries and rehiring them was to the ultimate benefit of the company, but the burden would have been on him to support this claim and he could well have failed. It might be the case that the company would do better economically by moving to another part of the country where wages are lower. The requirement that corporations act in the interests of maximizing profits might have prevented him from acting as he did, despite the fact that his actions were generally held in high esteem, and *even if it could be shown that the shareholders would have approved of his actions.*

Daniel Greenwood explains that corporate law requires managers to act with the single-minded goal of maximizing profit. This is presumed to be the goal of shareholders. As Greenwood argues, however, very few – if any – shareholders are this single-minded. Requiring corporate managers to further an end not shared by actual shareholders forces businesses to act in ways that no one wants.[29]

In his class on business organizations, Greenwood posits a hypothetical situation in which a manager of a restaurant, Mr. Popper, wishes to serve African-American customers. The time is the 1950s. The shareholders agree with the manager's goal. However, it is clear that the white customers do not and, if the restaurant serves African Americans, the corporation's profits will decrease because the white customers will go elsewhere. Current corporate law would require the manager to maximize corporate profits even though neither the manager nor the shareholders want to do so. Greenwood's students conclude that current corporate law requires the manager to maximize corporate profits by excluding customers on the ground of race. Greenwood comments: "In short, they conclude that Mr. Popper should take an action they believe is wrong, and that they believe Mr. Popper believes is wrong, in order to promote the interests of third parties – who, as it happens, also believe the action is wrong."[30] Such are the ironies of the law of ownership. *But it does not have to be this way.* Nothing in the fact of ownership requires this.

When Robert Monks observed pollution in a stream in Maine, he realized that, although no one wanted this to happen, it nonetheless had happened because the structure of corporate governance had induced companies to act in ways that caused the pollution, even though such pollution would ultimately not be in the interests of either the corporation or the public at large. Maximizing the firm's profits at all costs induces the firm to externalize harmful effects, including environmental pollution, onto others. But, as both Monks and Nell Minow report, ultimately the corporation will bear these costs, as well.[31]

The stakeholder laws adopted in the majority of states allow managers to take into account the interests of a wide variety of stakeholders who have an ongoing interest in the well-being of the corporate enterprise. These stakeholders include workers, creditors, and the communities in which the corporation operates. However, these statutes do not give any of the protected groups a right to sue to protect their interests; thus case law that could constrain the discretion of managers will not develop. In the absence of other mechanisms to ensure that the interests of workers and communities are given their due weight along with the interests of shareholders, these laws may do more harm than good. They may, for example, give managers too much discretion to consider a wide range of conflicting interests, and thereby allow them to further their own interests, rather than the interests of those they are legally obligated to serve. Giving managers a clear goal constrains their discretion and makes them act in a manner that furthers the interests of a constituency other than themselves. At the same time, if the goal is too precisely limited – such as the single-minded maximization of the value of shares – corporate law may induce managers to act in a manner that is not in anyone's interest.

Institutional investors, such as pension funds, own about half the publicly held stock in the United States. It has been argued that such investors are more likely to take a long-range view and to understand that they are harmed as well as benefited by corporate practices such as environmental pollution.[32] Action by such investors to control corporate management may induce corporate managers to do a better job of balancing interests in profit maximization against interests in preventing discrimination or environmental degradation.

It is not at all clear, however, that those institutional investors who do become active in shaping corporate policy adequately represent the interests of those affected by their decisions. They may be as zealously profit oriented as traditional corporate law assumed. Indeed, current federal law generally requires pension funds to maximize returns to plan beneficiaries. As we have seen, inflexible dedication to profit maximization may induce companies to act in ways that harm the public – and ultimately, the plan beneficiaries themselves. Democratizing control of investment funds may allow more debates about the appropriate directions of corporate policy, pushing managers to balance interests in profit against such interests as good employee or community relations. This goal will be a hard one to achieve, however, given the dispersed ownership structure of such funds.

Another approach is to give employees a greater say in how large corporations are run. After all, employees rely on continued access to their jobs, are (paradoxically) less movable than factories, and have a greater interest in the continued success of a particular corporate enterprise than shareholders who invest in diversified funds. Precisely because so much of an employee's interests are tied up in a particular company, giving employees greater say in corporate decisions might balance the instability generated by global competition for investment dollars. A number of European countries, including the Scandinavian countries and Germany, give workers the right to sit on the board of directors or to participate in "works councils." These approaches may force the board to balance the interests of shareholders against the interests of workers and lead to consideration of a more balanced range of values. They may also lead corporations to give greater weight to community and worker interests in job stability and satisfaction.

Perhaps the best way to give employees greater control over their lives is to make them part owners of the company for which they work. This can be done by expansion and revision of employee stock ownership plans (ESOPs). Most ESOPs do not give employees voting rights, making them owners in terms of value but not in terms of control. Employees could also be given more control over their own pension funds, which are the major owners of corporate stock in the country.[33]

Employees who have both stock ownership and voting rights in their own company would be better empowered to exercise voice, as well as exit, in determining company policy. There is a downside, of course. Putting more of an employee's wealth in a particular company means that there is even greater risk in losing one's wealth as compared to a situation in which the employee owns stock in many companies. One needs to balance the benefits of control rights against the security provided by diverse stock ownership. As is the usual case today, however, the lack of employee ownership in their own companies leaves employees vulnerable because their interests in continued employment are not represented on the board of directors.

At the very least, the courts should interpret stakeholder laws to authorize corporate managers to do what Feuerstein did – reinvest in the company, preserve jobs, help maintain a stable community – when the company is profitable. The law pertaining to the ownership and management of corporations should include incentives that encourage managers to consider legitimate aspects of the public interest as well as the interests of shareholders. Managers should also be induced to assume more realistic attitudes toward shareholder interests. The law should recognize that economic profit is not anyone's only goal in life. How to better balance competing interests in profit and job security, flexibility and stability, efficiency and human dignity, property and democracy is a complicated policy question. In trying to formulate public policy, we should take into account two things in particular that are often missing from current discussions of economic policy.

First, employees have strong interests in having a voice about their daily work lives. Those interests should be recognized and protected. Workers have substantive interests in job security and in the terms and conditions of employment. With the decrease in union membership and the practice of downsizing, current business and labor practices do not adequately protect those interests.

Second, communities have interests in stability. This does not mean that plants should never close or relocate. It does mean that the legal system should consider how corporate decisions affect not only their shareholders but entire communities. Our current system does not adequately protect the interests of communities. Property protects stability in order to free us to live as human beings should be entitled to live. If this is so, then the interests of workers and communities in job stability, and in access to new jobs when stability is not possible, are entitled to at least as much consideration as the protection now granted to the interests of shareholders. Of course, communities, businesses, and individual workers all have interests in flexibility, as well as stability. How to accomplish this balance is a difficult question.

What is important, however, is realization that the goal of providing stability to workers and access to employment when such stability is not possible is the *same goal* as the goal underlying property law: protecting the security that is necessary for human liberty to flourish. The choice is not between regulation and property but between protecting the interests of some people in stable access to resources and protecting all people. Objections to legal protections for jobholders and communities are thus objections to recognizing property rights. Paradoxical as it may sound, the institution of property requires public policies that protect those in need of security as much as those who already have it.

The Entrance to the Tent

Abraham was renowned for his hospitality. The Torah tells us that he sat at "the entrance to his tent at the heat of the day" (Gen. [*Bereishit*] 18:1). Why on earth would he do that on a hot day rather than sitting inside where it would be cooler? The rabbis tell us he was looking for travelers; he was seeking others who might need his aid and who might be shy about asking for help. Suddenly he saw three strangers, in the desert, far from home. "When he saw them, he *ran* to meet them from the entrance to his tent" (Gen. [*Bereishit*] 18:2). When they accepted his offer of food and drink, he "*hastened* into his tent" to ask Sarah to prepare the food, he "*ran* to the oxen" and gave the ox to his servant so he might "*hasten* to make it ready." (Gen. [*Bereishit*] 18:1–8) He rushed to receive them; he rushed to give them food. Our teachers tell us that all this running and hastening at the height of the day's heat in the desert is intended to show the importance of the obligation to be kind to strangers.

These strangers turned out to be angels (*malachim*) and messengers of God. The story reminds us that each person was created in the image of God, just as the street people in Larson's play *Rent* remind us that Christmas bells should ring as much for them as for anyone else. Each one counts and no one can be left out.

Notes

References to *WL* signify citations from Westlaw, an online legal research tool at www.westlaw.com.

Introduction

1. *State v. Shack,* 277 A.2d 369, 372 (N.J. 1971).

2. Cheryl Russell and Margaret Ambry, *The Official Guide to American Incomes* (Ithaca, N.Y.: New Strategist Publications and Consulting, 1993), 278. Those standards are not generous. The official poverty line is far below the amount necessary to sustain a minimally decent lifestyle. "In 1994 the American public responded to the Roper poll that it took a family of four about $25,000 just to get by; the federal poverty line for a family of four for that year stood at about $15,000." John E. Schwarz, *Illusions of Opportunity: The American Dream in Question* (New York: W. W. Norton, 1997), 63.

3. Jedediah Purdy, *For Common Things: Irony, Trust, and Commitment in America Today* (New York: Alfred A. Knopf, 1999), 180.

4. See generally Carol M. Rose, *Property and Persuasion: Essays on the History, Theory, and Rhetoric of Ownership* (Boulder, Colo.: Westview Press, 1994).

Chapter One: UNCOMMON DECENCY

1. Hillel, quoted in Shlomo P. Toperoff, *Avot [Pirkei Avot]: A Comprehensive Commentary on the Ethics of the Fathers* (Northvale, N.J.: Jason Aronson, 1997), *perek 5, mishnah 13,* p. 312 (my translation of the original Hebrew).

2. Avivah Gottlieb Zornberg, *Genesis: The Beginning of Desire* (Philadelphia: Jewish Publication Society, 1995/5755), 378.

3. Josh Simon, "Heroes of the Moment: The Mensch of Malden Mills: When Fire Destroyed a Mill and Threatened the Jobs of His Workers, Aaron Feuerstein Heeded an Ancient Rabbinic Teaching: 'Where there is no man, be a man,'" *Life,* May 5, 1997, 4A. 1997 WL 8498482.

4. Bruce Butterfield, "Mill Owner Feuerstein Vows to Pay Idled Workers for another day," *Boston Globe,* Feb. 10, 1996, 58, 1996 WL 6849522.

5. Bruce Butterfield, "Lawrence Will Mark Malden Mills Rebirth: Complex Destroyed in December 1995 Fire," *Boston Globe,* Sept. 13, 1997, F2, 1997 WL 6269327; "Malden Mills Rebuilt in Inner City," *Dallas Morning News,* Sept. 13, 1997, 11F, 1997 WL 11520076.

6. Bruce Butterfield, "Malden Mills to Cut 300 Jobs in Velvet Unit: Vows to Rehire Workers Within Two Years," *Boston Globe,* Feb. 26, 1998, D1.

7. Simon, "Heroes of the Moment," 4A.

8. Laura Meade Kirk, "Museum Offers Lesson in Value of Work: Aaron Feuerstein, Who Kept His Employees on the Payroll When His Malden Mills Plant Burned Down, Tells Hundreds at a New Woonsocket Museum that Urban Employment Is Essential for the Financial Health of the Nation," *Providence Journal-Bulletin,* Oct. 13, 1997, B01, 1997 WL 13863537.

9. Samuel Heilman, "Looking In: A Shining Example of Orthodoxy; Selfless New England Mill Owner Helps Atone for Transgressions by His Coreligionists," *Jewish Week,* Feb. 2, 1996, 24, 1996 WL 15747037.

10. Ibid.

11. David Nyhan, "The Mensch Who Saved Christmas," *Boston Globe,* Dec. 17, 1995, A20, 1995 WL 5966820.

12. "Mill Workers Call Jewish Boss Santa," *Charleston Daily Mail,* Dec. 25, 1995, 05A, 1995 WL 13226009.

13. Laurie Loisel, "Mill owner discounts heroism in local talk," *Daily Hampshire Gazette,* Nov. 21, 1996, 1, 1996 WL 8549945.

14. Edward D. Murphy, "Honored Businessman Decries Values of Today's Corporate World: Mill Owner Aaron Feuerstein Tells an Audience in Portland that Loyalty Pays Off Over the Long Term," *Portland Press Herald,* Dec. 4, 1997, 1A, 1997 WL12537662.

15. Robert Charles Clark, *Corporate Law* § 3.1.2 at 96 (Little, Brown, 1986) (shareholders have the power to sue managers for breach of their duty of loyalty

to shareholders); Robert A. G. Monks and Nell Minow, *Corporate Governance* (Cambridge, Mass.: Blackwell Publishers, 1995), 182 (corporate directors owe shareholder/owners legally enforceable duties of loyalty and care).

16. Feuerstein explained: "I own my company, but it's unfortunate that CEOs, who are maybe professionally far better than me, are being forced today, because of [the] power in the hands of these Wall Street funds, they're being forced today to make short-term decisions to improve the bottom line. As a result of it, they are cutting and killing the very labor that this country needs for its future." "Profile: No Longer Needed: Aaron Feuerstein, Corporate America's Layoff Policies, and How They Affect the United States," *Sunday Morning,* Jan. 14, 1996 (CBS, transcript), 1996 WL 8065770.

17. Roberto Mangabeira Unger, *Democracy Realized: The Progressive Alternative* (New York: Verso, 1998), 44.

18. Rebecca M. Blank, *It Takes a Nation: A New Agenda for Fighting Poverty* (Princeton, N.J.: Princeton University Press, 1997). John E. Schwarz argues that the official poverty line is far below the amount necessary to sustain a minimally decent lifestyle. "In 1994 the American public responded to the Roper poll that it took a family of four about $25,000 just to get by; the federal poverty line for a family of four for that year stood at about $15,000." John E. Schwarz, *Illusions of Opportunity: The American Dream in Question* (New York: W. W. Norton, 1997), 63. Moreover, Schwarz argues that not enough good jobs exist to enable families to obtain a minimally decent lifestyle. He estimates that the shortage of good jobs leaves roughly 15.7 million households out in the cold (p. 74).

19. Richard Sennett, *The Corrosion of Character: The Personal Consequences of Work in the New Capitalism* (New York: W. W. Norton, 1998), 146.

20. Ibid.

21. Mary Jo Bane and David T. Ellwood, *Welfare Realities: From Rhetoric to Reform* (Cambridge Harvard University Press, 1994); Blank, *It Takes a Nation;* Sheldon H. Danziger, Gary D. Sandefur, and Daniel H. Weinberg, eds., *Confronting Poverty: Prescriptions for Change* (Cambridge: Harvard University Press, 1994); Charles Derber, *Corporation Nation: How Corporations Are Taking Over Our Lives and What We Can Do About It* (New York: St. Martin's Press, 1998); Lisa Dodson, *Don't Call Us Out of Name: The Untold Lives of Women and Girls in Poor America* (Boston: Beacon Press, 1998); David T. Ellwood, *Poor Support:*

Poverty in the American Family (New York: Basic Books, 1988); James K. Galbraith, *Created Unequal: The Crisis in American Pay* (New York: Free Press, 1998); Joel F. Handler and Yeheskel Hasenfeld, *We the Poor People* (New Haven: Yale University Press, 1997); Christopher Jencks, *Rethinking Social Policy: Race, Poverty, and the Underclass* (Cambridge Harvard University Press, 1992); Douglas S. Massey and Nancy A. Denton, *American Apartheid: Segregation and the Making of the Underclass* (Cambridge Harvard University Press, 1993); Gwendolyn Mink, *Welfare's End* (Ithaca, N.Y.: Cornell University Press, 1998); Brendan O'Flaherty, *Making Room: The Economics of Homelessness* (Cambridge: Harvard University Press, 1996); Katherine S. Newman, *Falling from Grace: The Experience of Downward Mobility in the American Middle Class* (New York: Free Press, 1988); Katherine S. Newman, *No Shame in My Game: The Working Poor in the Inner City* (New York: Alfred A. Knopf and Russell Sage Foundation 1999); Schwarz, *Illusions of Opportunity;* Sennett, *Corrosion of Character;* Judith N. Shklar, *American Citizenship* (Cambridge: Harvard University Press, 1991); Robert M. Solow et al., *Work and Welfare,* ed. Amy Gutmann (Princeton, N.J.: Princeton University Press, 1998); William Julius Wilson, *The Truly Disadvantaged: The Inner City, the Underclass, and Public Policy* (Chicago: University of Chicago Press, 1987); William Julius Wilson, *When Work Disappears: The World of the New Urban Poor* (New York: Alfred A. Knopf, 1996); Unger, *Democracy Realized;* Robert Mangabeira Unger and Cornel West, *The Future of American Progressivism* (Boston: Beacon Press, 1998); Edward N. Wolff, *Top Heavy: The Increasing Inequality of Wealth in America and What Can Be Done About It* (New York: New Press, 1996).

22. Robert Kuttner, *Everything for Sale: The Virtues and Limits of Markets* (New York: Alfred A. Knopf, 1998).

23. For a recent argument to that effect, see Richard Pipes, *Property and Freedom* (New York: Alfred A. Knopf, 1999).

24. Alex Poinsett, "Economic Apartheid Haunts South Africa," *Chicago Tribune,* May 18, 1998, 15, 1998 WL 2857246.

Chapter Two: OUTSIDE THE BOUNDARIES

1. Clifton Fadiman, ed., *The Little, Brown Book of Anecdotes* (Boston: Little, Brown, 1985), 395.

2. Gregory S. Alexander, *Commodity and Propriety: Competing Visions of*

Property in American Legal Thought 1776–1970 (Chicago; University of Chicago Press, 1997), 1–2.

3. *People ex rel. Moloney v. Pullman's Palace-Car Co.,* 51 N.E. 664, 674 (Ill. 1898).

4. Robert Kuttner, *Everything for Sale: The Virtues and Limits of Markets* (New York: Alfred A. Knopf, 1998), 86.

5. 236 U.S. 1, 17 (1915).

6. Jedediah Purdy, *For Common Things: Irony, Trust, and Commitment in America Today* (New York: Alfred A. Knopf, 1999), 131.

7. See Michael Walzer, *Radical Principles: Reflections of an Unreconstructed Democrat* (New York: Basic Books, 1980), 273–90.

8. *Imperial Colliery Co. v. Fout,* 373 S.E. 2d 489 (W. Va. 1988).

9. For a contemporary version of this kind of controversy, consider the dispute over the town called Celebration, constructed, owned, and managed by Walt Disney Company. Douglas Frantz and Catherine Collins, *Celebration, U.S.A.: Living in Disney's Brave New Town* (New York: Henry Holt, 1999); Andrew Ross, *The Celebration Chronicles: Life, Liberty, and the Pursuit of Property Value* (New York: Ballantine Books, 1999).

10. *Van Rensselaer v. Hays,* 19 N.Y. 68 (1859).

11. Marylynn Salmon, *Women and the Law of Property in Early America* (Chapel Hill, N. C.: University of North Carolina Press, 1986), 14–40.

12. Reva B. Siegel, "Home as Work: The First Woman's Rights Claims Concerning Wives' Household Labor," *Yale Law Journal* 103 (1994): 1073; Reva B. Siegel, "The Modernization of Marital Status Law: Adjudicating Wives' Rights to Earnings, 1850–1880," *Georgetown Law Journal* 82 (1994): 2127.

13. *Kirchberg v. Feenstra,* 450 U.S. 455 (1981).

14. Roberto Mangabeira Unger, *Democracy Realized: The Progressive Alternative* (New York: Verso, 1998), 49.

15. Jeremy Waldron, "Homelessness and the Issue of Freedom," *UCLA Law Review* 39 (1991): 295.

16. Jeremy Waldron, *The Right to Private Property* (Oxford: Clarendon Press, 1988), 329, 5.

17. Laura S. Underkuffler-Freund, "Property: A Special Right," *Notre Dame Law Review* 71 (1996): 1033, 1038.

18. Ibid.

19. John Locke, *The Second Treatise of Government,* ed. Oscar Piest (Indianapolis, Ind.: Bobbs-Merrill, 1952), 18–30.

20. *City of Chicago v. Morales,* – U.S. – , 119 S.Ct. 1849, 67 U.S.L.W. 4415 (1999).

21. *Pottinger v. City of Miami,* 810 F.Supp. 1551 (S. D.Fla. 1992).

22. Waldron, *Homelessness,* 295, 296.

23. Richard Sennett, *The Corrosion of Character: The Personal Consequences of Work in the New Capitalism* (New York: W. W. Norton, 1998), 146.

24. John E. Schwarz, *Illusions of Opportunity: The American Dream in Question* (New York: W. W. Norton, 1997), 73.

25. James K. Galbraith, *Created Unequal: The Crisis in American Pay* (New York: Free Press, 1998).

26. Thomas Hobbes, *Leviathan* (Harmondsworth, U.K.: Penguin Books, 1968), 186.

27. John Locke, *The Second Treatise of Government* (Indianapolis, Ind.: Bobbs-Merrill, 1952), 70.

28. Kuttner, *Everything for Sale,* 73–77.

29. Kent Greenfield, "The Unjustified Absence of Federal Fraud Protection in the Labor Market," *Yale Law Journal* 107 (1997), 715.

30. Ibid. See also *Local 1330, United Steel Workers of America v. United States Steel Corp.,* 631 F.2d 1264 (6th Cir. 1980).

Chapter Three: THE EDGES OF THE FIELD

1. Everett Fox, trans., *The Five Books of Moses* (New York: Schocken Books, 1995), 631.

2. The Hebrew source for this quotation is Shlomo P. Toperoff, ed., *Avot: A Comprehensive Commentary on the Ethics of the Fathers* (Northvale, N.J.: Jason Aronson, 1997, 312 my English translation).

3. Patricia Smith, "Deaths Mar Our Fantasy World," *Boston Globe,* Dec. 15, 1997, B1.

4. Stephanie Ebbert, "Deadly Period for Homeless Is Troubling Activists: 6 Lives Lost Since Middle of December," *Boston Globe,* Jan. 28, 1998, B2, 1998 WL 9114613.

5. Stephanie Ebbert, "Homeless Mourn One of Their Own: Memorial Service Held on Common," *Boston Globe,* Dec. 12, 1997, B2, 1997 WL 6284976.

6. Stephanie Ebbert, "Homeless Man Found Dead on Park Bench Downtown," *Boston Globe,* Dec. 13, 1998, B6, 1998 WL 22239501.

7. Francie Latour, "A Cold Night, a Life Ended on Common: Homeless Man Found Frozen Beneath Tree," *Boston Globe,* Dec. 11, 1997, B1, 1997 WL 6284851.

8. Ebbert, "Homeless Man Found Dead."

9. Robert Frost, "The Death of the Hired Man," quoted in Louis Untermeyer, *A Concise Treasury of Great Poems* (New York: Pocket Books, 1942), 433–34.

10. Majid Fakhry, trans., *The Qur'an: A Modern English Version* (Reading, U.K.: Garnet Publishing, 1997), 414.

11. Gregory S. Alexander, *Commodity and Propriety* (Chicago: University of Chicago Press, 1997), 26–42.

12. They include *Baba Qamma, Baba Mesia,* and *Baba Batra.* See Jacob Neusner, trans., *The Mishnah: A New Translation* (New Haven: Yale University Press, 1988), 528–57.

13. "Violence:" Gen. (*Bereishit*) 6:11, in A. M. Silbermann, ed., *Chumash, with Targum Onkelos, Haphtaroth and Rashi's Commentary* (Jerusalem: Silbermann Family, 1934/5745); *The Torah: The Five Books of Moses,* 3d ed. (Philadelphia and Jerusalem: Jewish Publication Society, 1992). "Lawlessness:" Gen. (*Bereishit*) 6:11, in W. Gunther Plaut, ed., *The Torah: A Modern Commentary* (New York: Union of American Hebrew Congregations, 1981). "Wrongdoing:" Gen. (*Bereishit*) 6:11, in Everett Fox, trans., *The Five Books of Moses* (New York: Schocken Books, 1995). "Outrage:" Gen. (*Bereishit*) 6:11, in Robert Alter, trans., *Genesis: Translation and Commentary* (New York: W. W. Norton, 1996).

14. Gen. (*Bereishit*) 6:6, in Fox, *Five Books of Moses.*

15. Rashi is Rabbi Schlomo Yitzkhaki (1040–1105), generally understood as the greatest commentator on the Torah.

16. Rashi, Commentary to Gen. 6:11, in Silbermann, *Chumash,* 28.

17. Silbermann, *Chumash,* 28; Rashi, quoted in Avivah Gottlieb Zornberg, *Genesis: The Beginning of Desire* (Philadelphia: Jewish Publication Society, 5755/1995), 51.

18. Ibid.

19. Zornberg, *Genesis,* 51.

20. Meir Tamari, *The Challenge of Wealth: A Jewish Perspective on Earning and Spending Money* (Northvale, N.J.: Jason Aronson, 1995), 36.

21. Zornberg, *Genesis,* 51 (my emphasis); Silbermann, *Chumash,* 28.

22. Zornberg, *Genesis,* 51.

23. Ibid., 52.

24. Ibid., 52–53.

25. Ibid., 41, 59–64.

26. Ibid., 60–61.

27. Tamari, *Challenge of Wealth,* 128.

28. Deut. (*D'varim*) 15:8, 11; 14:29; 14:27.

29. Tamari, *Challenge of Wealth,* xxiii.

30. Exo. (*Shemot*) 23:9.

31. Tamari, *Challenge of Wealth,* 128.

32. Ezek. 16:49–50.

33. Tamari, *Challenge of Wealth,* 148.

34. Tamari, *Challenge of Wealth,* 167.

35. Ibid., 170–71.

36. Tamari, *Challenge of Wealth,* 170.

37. Lev. (*Vayikra*) 23:22. See Tamari, *Challenge of Wealth,* 132–34.

38. Lev. (*Vayikra*) 19:9–10, 23:22; Deut. (*D'varim*) 24:20–21. See Tamari, *Challenge of Wealth,* 156.

39. Deut. (*D'varim*) 24:19.

40. For a Christian perspective on the "edges of the field," see Jim Wallis, *The Soul of Politics: Beyond "Religious Right" and "Secular Left"* (New York: Harcourt Brace, 1995), 200.

41. S. Rabinowitz, trans, *7 Midrash Rabbah: Ruth* (New York: Soncino Press, 1983), xii; 8–9; Avivah Zornberg, "The Concealed Alternative," in *Reading Ruth: Contemporary Women Reclaim a Sacred Story,* Judith A. Kates and Gail Twersky Reimer, eds. (New York: Ballantine Books, 1994), 65, 70–71.

42. *Talmud Bavli, Baba Batra* 21b, quoted in Tamari, *Challenge of Wealth,* 72.

43. Tamari, *Challenge of Wealth,* 74–75.

44. Maimonides, *Mishneh Torah, Hilkhot De'ot,* ch. 5, halakhah 13, quoted in ibid., 135.

45. Tamari, *Challenge of Wealth,* 53–61.

46. Ibid., 52.

47. Ibid., 53.

48. Josh Simon, "Heroes of the Moment: The Mensch of Malden Mills; When Fire Destroyed a Mill and Threatened the Jobs of His Workers, Aaron Feuerstein Heeded an Ancient Rabbinic Teaching: 'Where there is no man, be a man,'" *Life,* May 5, 1997, 4A, 1997 WL 8498482.

49. Tamari, *Challenge of Wealth,* 37–39.

50. *Talmud Bavli, Sanhedrin* 108a, quoted in ibid., 38.

51. Aaron Kirschenbaum, *Equity in Jewish Law: Beyond Equity: Halakhic Aspirationism in Jewish Civil Law* (New York: Yeshiva University Press, 1991), 109–36.

52. Tamari, *Challenge of Wealth,* 109.

53. Ibid., 120; Kirschenbaum, *Equity in Jewish Law,* 127.

54. "Tractate Bava Metzia," Part iii (44a), in *The Talmud: The Steinsaltz Edition,* vol. 3, Adin Steinsaltz, ed. (New York: Random House, 1990), 6.

55. Milner S. Ball, *The Word and the Law* (Chicago: University of Chicago Press, 1993), 111.

56. National Conference of Catholic Bishops, *Economic Justice for All: Pastoral Letter on Catholic Social Teaching and the U.S. Economy* (Washington, D.C.: United States Catholic Conference, 1986), vi. See also Wallis, *Soul of Politics,* 83.

57. Catholic Bishops, *Economic Justice for All,* x.

58. Ibid., ix–x.

59. Wallis, *Soul of Politics,* 84.

60. Catholic Bishops, *Economic Justice for All,* 23–24.

61. Ibid., 37.

62. Ibid., 39.

63. Ibid., 42.

64. Anthony E. Cook, *The Least of These: Race, Law, and Religion in American Culture* (New York: Routledge, 1997), 95.

65. Ibid., 114.

66. Martin Luther King, Jr., *The Trumpet of Conscience,* quoted in Ibid., 122.

67. William Stringfellow, *My People Is the Enemy: An Autobiographical Polemic* (New York: Holt, Rinehart, and Winston, 1964), 38.

68. Peter J. Gomes, *The Good Book: Reading the Bible with Mind and Heart* (New York: Avon Books, 1996), 287, 306–8.

69. Ibid., 298–99.

70. Ibid., 309.

71. Ibid., 299–300.

72. Wallis, *Soul of Politics,* 47.

73. Matt. 25:45, quoted in ibid., 83.

74. Wallis, *Soul of Politics,* 83.

75. Ibid., 179.

76. M. Cherif Bassiouni, *Introduction to Islam* (Washington, D.C.: American-Arab Affairs Council, 1985), 15; Neal Robinson, *Islam: A Concise Introduction* (Surrey, U.K.: Curzon Press, 1999), 113.

77. Shaikh Mahmud Ahmad, *Social Justice in Islam,* 2d ed. (Lahore, Pakistan: Institute of Islamic Culture, 1975), 79–114; Abd El-Razzak Nofal, *Al Zakat: "The Poor Due,"* trans. Mrs. Tomader Twefik (Cairo: Supreme Council for Islamic Affairs).

78. Akhtar Khan, *Zakat, Sadaqah, and Zakat-ul-Fitr* (Silver Spring, Md.: Muslim Community Center, n.d.) (http://www.erols.com/mccmd/zakat1. htm; visited Sept. 15, 1999).

79. Ibid.; Abdel Fattah Aly, *The Muslim Concept of Charity* (http://pages. prodigy.net/abboud/charity.htm; 1997–98); Robinson, *Islam,* 111.

80. Charis Waddy, *The Muslim Mind,* 3d ed. (Lanham, Md.: New Amsterdam Books, 1990), 42.

81. Bassiouni, *Introduction to Islam,* 43.

82. Robinson, *Islam,* 111–12.

83. Khan, *Zakat, Sadaqah, and Zakat-ul-Fitr.*

84. Ibid. See also "A person who is too poor to pay *zakat* is still required to act charitably" in Robinson, *Islam,* 113.

85. Robinson, *Islam,* 112–13.

86. Zornberg, *Genesis,* 203–4.

87. Ibid., 206.

88. Lev. (*Vayikra*) 25:10.

89. "Decency to the Rescue," *Phoenix Gazette,* Jan. 20, 1996, B6.

1. Jedediah Purdy, *For Common Things: Irony, Trust, and Commitment in America Today* (New York: Alfred A. Knopf, 1999), 109.

2. Jonathan Larson, "What You Own," on *Rent,* Dreamworks compact disk DRMD2-50003. All quotations from *Rent* are taken from this disk.

3. *The Full Monty* (Beverly Hills, Calif.: Twentieth Century Fox Home Entertainment 1997).

4. Roger Ebert, "Underneath It All, 'Full Monty' About Fight for Dignity," *Denver Post,* Mar. 20, 1998, F02, 1998 WL 6105826.

5. "Full Monty Outstrips the Lot," *Daily Mail,* June 10, 1999, 64, 1999 WL 19063244.

6. *Brassed Off* (New York: Miramax Films, 1997).

7. *New Shorter Oxford Dictionary* (Oxford: Clarendon Press, 1993), s.v. "redundancy."

8. *The Full Monty.*

9. *Brassed Off.*

10. Mark Knopfler (Dire Straits), "Telegraph Road," on *Love Over Gold,* Warner Bros. 9 23728–2.

11. Lynnley Browning, "Pieces Fall Together: Fleet, BankBoston Announce Second Round of Key Appointments," *Boston Globe,* May 11, 1999, D1, WL 6061712.

12. Lynn Browning, "Fleet, BankBoston Face Their Critics: Activists Ask for More Facts, Merger Delay," *Boston Globe,* July 8, 1999, A01.

13. *Brassed Off.*

14. *Big Business* (Burbank, Calif.: Touchstone Pictures/Buena Vista Home Video, 1987).

15. "The Measure of a Man," *Star Trek: The Next Generation* (Hollywood, Calif.: Paramount Pictures/Paramount Home Video, 1989).

16. Ibid.

17. Purdy, *Common Things,* 20.

18. "Yaakov [Jacob] rent his clothes,/he put sackloth on his loins/and mourned his son for many days." Gen. (*Bereishit*) 37:34, in Everett Fox, trans., *The Five Books of Moses* (New York: Schocken Books, 1995), 181.

19. Gen. (*Bereishit*) 37:33, in ibid. The Jewish Publication Society translation reads "Joseph was torn by a beast." *The Torah: The Five Books of Moses,* 3d.

ed. (Jewish Publication Society, 1992), 71. The verse reads: *Tarof toraf Yosef.* Joseph's name, *Yosef,* comes from the verb "to add." He was Rachel's first, long-awaited child, and she hoped God would add more children. But Joseph also "added" joy to the lives of Rachel and Jacob. Thus, the verse powerfully expresses the grief of Jacob (*Yaakov*) at the loss of his son. The one who tears tore apart the one who was to add. The gain, the incredible joy brought by the birth of the boy was torn away, torn to pieces. Life itself was ripped apart.

20. See generally Harold S. Kushner, *When Bad Things Happen to Good People,* 2d ed. (New York: Schocken Books, 1989).

21. Imbricate: a lovely, little-known word referring to biological or physical features of a design that overlap, as in tiles or shingles on a roof or the elements of a pine cone.

22. See Elizabeth V. Spelman, *Fruits of Sorrow: Framing Our Attention to Suffering* (Boston: Beacon Press, 1997), 23–25.

23. See generally Laura S. Underkuffler-Freund, "Property: A Special Right," *Notre Dame Law Review* 71 (1996), 1033.

24. Jim Wallis, *The Soul of Politics: Beyond "Religious Right" and "Secular Left"* (New York: Harcourt Brace, 1995), 84.

Chapter Five: COMMON DECENCY

1. Martha C. Nussbaum, *Poetic Justice: The Literary Imagination and Public Life* (Boston: Beacon Press, 1995), 25.

2. Kurt Vonnegut, Slapstick (New York: Dell Publishing, 1976), 5.

3. John Dewey, *Individualism – Old and New* (New York: Minton, Balch, 1930), 9, 12, 10.

4. Ibid., 11.

5. Ibid.

6. Ibid., 12–13.

7. Ibid., 13.

8. *State v. Shack,* 277 A.2d 369 (N.J. 1971).

9. Richard Sennett, *The Corrosion of Character: The Personal Consequences of Work in the New Capitalism* (New York: W. W. Norton, 1998), 147.

10. Jean Jacques Rousseau, "A Discourse on the Origin of Inequality," in *The Social Contract and Discourses,* trans. G. D. H. Cole (New York: E. P. Dutton, 1950), 175, 226.

11. Katherine S. Newman, *Falling from Grace: The Experience of Downward Mobility in the American Middle Class* (New York: Free Press, 1988).

12. Derrick Z. Jackson, "Creating, Not Curbing, Poverty," *Boston Globe,* Jan. 20, 1999, A15.

13. Doris Sue Wong, "Welfare Changes Lauded," *Boston Globe,* Feb. 25, 1999, B01 (reporting that only 75 percent of those who left welfare were working); Katherine S. Newman, *No Shame in My Game: The Working Poor in the Inner City* (New York: Alfred A. Knopf and Russell Sage Foundation 1999), 269.

14. Alan Brinkley, *The Unfinished Nation: A Concise History of the American People* (New York: Alfred A. Knopf, 1993), 695–96.

15. John E. Schwarz, *Illusions of Opportunity: The American Dream in Question* (New York: W. W. Norton, 1997), 63, 74.

16. Associated Press, "Parents of Many Poor Children Work, Welfare Researchers Say," *Boston Globe,* Feb. 25, 1999, A12.

17. Wong, "Welfare Changes Lauded" (reporting that only 75 percent of those who left welfare were working).

18. Sally Jacobs, "Better Food, a Room of Her Own: Welfare Reform, Through a Child's Eyes," *Boston Globe,* Jan. 24, 1999, B1, B6.

19. Katherine S. Newman, *No Shame in My Game,* 270–71.

20. Ibid., 275–76.

21. Matthew Brelis, "Helter Shelter: Housing Costs Are Out of Control. Does Anyone Care?" *Boston Globe,* Jan. 24, 1999, F1, F2.

22. Jason DeParle, "As Welfare Rolls Shrink, Load on Relatives Grows: Weary Milwaukee Grandmothers Tell of Strain," *New York Times,* Feb. 21, 1999, 1, 20.

23. Joel F. Handler and Yeheskel Hasenfeld, *We the Poor People: Work, Poverty, and Welfare* (New Haven: Yale University Press, 1997), 110–11; Gwendolyn Mink, *Welfare's End* (Ithaca, N.Y.: Cornell University Press, 1998).

24. Amy L. Wax, "Bargaining in the Shadow of the Market: Is There a Future for Egalitarian Marriage?" *Virginia Law Review* 84(1998), 509, 655.

25. Celia W. Dugger, "Iowa Plan Tries to Cut Off the Cash," *New York Times,* April 7, 1995, A1, quoted in Handler and Hasenfeld, *We the Poor People,* 98.

26. Joel F. Handler, "Welfare-to-Work: Reform or Rhetoric?" *Administrative Law Review* 50 (1998), 3.

27. Kent Greenfield, "The Unjustified Absence of Federal Fraud Protection in the Labor Market," *Yale Law Journal* 107 (1997), 715.

28. Kent Greenfield and John E. Nilsson, "Gradgrind's Education: Using Dickens and Aristotle to Understand (and Replace?) the Business Judgment Rule," *Brooklyn Law Review* 63 (1997), 799, 849–52.

29. Daniel J. H. Greenwood, "Fictional Shareholders: For Whom Are Corporate Managers Trustees, Revisited," *Southern California Law Review* 69 (1996), 1021.

30. Ibid., 1092.

31. Robert A. G. Monks and Nell Minow, *Power and Accountability* (New York: HarperCollins, 1991), 3.

32. Greenwood, *Fictional Shareholders,* 69.

33. Gregory S. Alexander, "Pensions and Passivity," *Law and Contemporary Problems* 56 (1993), 111.

Acknowledgments

I have had many teachers, but foremost among them have been my parents, Max and Lila Singer. I want to thank them from the bottom of my heart for all they have given me and all they have been to me. They were not only my first teachers but my emotional support and moral compass. I owe them more than I can say.

I have had other teachers as well, and I had a lot of help writing this book. Thanks and affection go to Martha Minow, Greg Alexander, Keith Aoki, Milner Ball, Larry Blum, Chris Desan, Stanley Frankel, Jerry Frug, Kent Greenfield, Jon Hanson, Todd Hinnen, Elinor Horne, Mort Horwitz, Duncan Kennedy, Larry Kramer, Rabbi Jonathan Kraus, Martha Mahoney, Josephine Minow, Nell Minow, Newton Minow, Jenny Nedelsky, Jeremy Paul, Avery Rimer, Florence Wagman Roisman, Fred Rowley, Bob Singer, Lila Singer, Max Singer, Judy Smith, Avi Soifer, Vicky Spelman, Carol Steiker, Nomi Stoltzenberg, Laura Underkuffler-Freund, André van der Walt, Johan van der Walt, Lucie White, Eric Yamamoto. I especially want to thank Patricia Fazzone for her expert administrative assistance and for her insights on the connections between spirituality and the work of the world.

Elizabeth V. Spelman has taught me about everyday joys and the possibility of repair. Mira Judith Minow Singer continues to astonish me with her stories, her questions, and her compassion. Martha Minow has shared with me her vision, her sensitivity, her imagination, and her uncanny ability to organize and clarify other people's ideas (including my own). She has made all the difference to me.

A different version of the material on *Rent* in chapter 4 was originally published in the *Boston College Law Review* 39 (1997): 1.

My friend Marcel Pallais (ל"ז) dedicated his life to "heal[ing] the suffering of incomplete existence."* After a Jesuit education in Nicaragua, he came to college in the United States. In a better world, he would have been a philosophy professor. He would have been a good one. In the world we know, he felt impelled to prepare to participate in the political transformation of his country. He studied economics, as well as philosophy, because he knew that a leader must be practical as well as visionary. Yet he would have been the first to say that philosophy, as he understood it, was eminently practical.

Marcel could have lived a comfortable, academic life, but he chose to return to Nicaragua and to work underground against his uncle's dictatorship. When the old regime fell, he entered the new government. Assigned to investigate economic fraud and torture in the old regime, he placed himself in grave danger. He was assassinated at the age of twenty-four while trying to help a family friend. The moral and religious teachings of his youth informed his understanding of both economics and philosophy. Marcel believed that it was possible for an economic and political system to respect liberty while promoting both equality and democracy. There is some evidence to believe that he was right, or so I hope. This book is dedicated to him.

Cambridge, Massachusetts
5760/2000

* Marcel H. Pallais Checa, *Sketches on Hegel's Science* (B.A. thesis, Williams College, 1977) (on file in the Langdell Library of Harvard Law School), ii.